MJ Magazine

VOLUME I • ISSUE 2

The Magazine Created by Authors for Authors

Fran Lewis, Founder

PUBLISHED BY FIDELI PUBLISHING INC..

ISBN: 978-1-60414-763-6

Fideli Publishing Inc.
119 W. Morgan St.
Martinsville, IN 46151

www.FideliPublishing.com

Dedicated to Marcia Joyce with love from Frani.

TABLE OF CONTENTS

THIS MAGAZINE IS SUPPORTED BY THE FOLLOWING BUSINESSES:

Luigi Of Italy

Address: 804 Allerton Ave, Bronx, NY 10467
Phone:(718) 655-4700
Owner: Tony

Enrico's Bakery – Hartsdale

Address: 214 East Hartsdale Ave., Hartsdale, New York 10530
Hours: 6:30 am - 8:00 pm
Phone: 914-723 0340
Owner: Joseph Floriano

Hartsdale Hair Studio

Address: 4 E. Hartsdale Ave., Hartsdale, NY 10530
Hours: Mon–Sat — 9:00am - 6:00pm Sunday's 10:00am–2:00pm By Appointment
Owner: Evelyn
Phone: 914-437-7811

C&C Coffee Shop and Deli

The best food in the Bronx at reasonable prices.

Address: 2438 Eastchester Road, Bronx, N.Y. 10469
Cuisine: Spanish, Italian, and American Cuisine
Catering available for All Occasions
Phone: 347 346 9824/ or 25
Owner: Carlos Ramero

Astor Prime Meat Market

Address: 1117 Astor Ave., Bronx, NY 10469
Phone: (718) 882-1177
Owner: Michael

Gennaro's Pizza

Address: 759 Central Park Ave, Scarsdale NY 10583
Phone: (914) 472-6329
Owner: John

My sister, Marcia Joyce, had an amazing personality, and she enjoyed making everyone smile. But, one of the greatest things we did together as sisters and best friends was write poems to everyone in the family for birthdays, anniversaries, and special occasions. Every year, my sister would call me in June to remind me that the holiday party she coordinated for her office was just months away. She was reminding me that we needed to get started writing the twenty-stanza poem she would read there and say she wrote.

We wrote this poem together:

If We All Joined Hands

By Fran Lewis & Marcia Joyce

I hope this poem is an inspiration to you and your fellow troop members.

If we all joined hands and formed a large circle,
If we all joined hands and smiled at each other,
What a huge circle it would be you would not believe your eyes,
Forming one large ring of each sister and each brother.

Living together and understanding our strengths and differences, you see,
Would help make the world a better place to live in for you and for me.
If we all joined hands and looked into each other's faces,
Smiled and hugged our neighbors who came from different place.

What a huge ring of love and hope this would be, and how far around it would go.
A never-ending circle of goodness and kindness for the entire world to know.
If we all joined hands and tried to understand one another,
Wouldn't that be great if did not use hate against each other?

Instead we would all pray that one day we could live in a world you know,
Free of strife, wars, and dissention, and people whose understanding would grow.
To see the world as it really is, with so many people in it who care,
To join their hands and show that our world is special beyond compare.

NOTES FROM FRAN

Fran Lewis

To My Precious Sister Marcia:

You filled my life with meaning and joy. You were, and still are, the one person who understood me and helped guide us both through the good times and the bad. Your smile and unique hello lit up a room and warmed the hearts of everyone that you met. As you go on your next journey, remember that you are not alone. Let the memories and fond recollections of our life together keep you strong and safe. Let there be memories that you will carry with you of all of your loved ones, and let them remain near in spirit, knowing that you will receive a tender, surprising, heartwarming welcome to the after world, and your spirit and love will live on for eternity. May the memories of those who loved and adored you surround you always and bring you comfort. You are a beacon of hope and joy for our family. Whenever I get stuck I will stop, think, and remember: To figure it out! I love you now and forever.

Your sister, and best pal, and best friend,
Frani

BE FLEXIBLE WITH YOUR PLOTTING

by Mark Bouton

As a mystery novel writer, I've often been asked whether I outline my plots. The answer is yes, and no. That is, when I began writing my first novel, I knew nothing about structure and plotting except what I had picked up subconsciously from reading numerous novels. So, I decided I should develop a skeleton upon which to build my story.

At first, I tried making an outline as to what would happen and when.

It was in the format of a bracket or sort of branching structure from one line to other lines beneath it. I suppose it worked, as I did finish the novel, eventually. And it only took me eight years.

Frankly, the writing of the first draft only took two years or so. Then I had to learn enough about the proper craftsmanship of the various elements of writing such as dialogue, description, and action to be able to rewrite the book enough times to make it marketable. I also learned, through numerous rejections and subsequent study, how to write an agent query well enough to land an agent.

Then I had to write a second novel. I will say that by plowing through your manuscript all the way through a first effort, you do develop a sense of pattern in your head that helps you navigate through subsequent books with much more assurance and confidence. But I did decide to continue to outline in writing my second attempt at a novel, as well.

In fact, I used a much more elaborate procedure to organize my next book. I bought a 2'x3' corkboard, a pack of colored markers, and some computer paper in order to make a sort of storyboard for my novel. I even showed where color-coded subplots appeared in the various chapters, so I'd be sure they were advancing on an even keel. Maybe I got a bit rigid in this case. But I did finish and sell the novel.

From then on, I decided I wouldn't use a strict outline per se. I did use a system of 3x5 index cards on which I'd write two or three sentences as to what would happen in each chapter. That seemed to work well for me, and I sometimes continue to use it today.

With a mystery novel, as with most works of fiction, the overall structure consists of a beginning, middle, and an end to complete the story. In this genre, that would amount to a crime being shown, followed by a series of investigative steps to develop clues leading toward a solution to the crime, and a putting together of those clues in order to identify, locate and arrest the criminal.

One situation that does occur on occasion is that a character comes alive and refuses to do some type of action or demands to do another. This can lead to an unplanned detour in your storyline. A minor character may need to become a major character. Or, you may have to change your idea of the original character altogether, giving him different physical or mental capabilities, or changing his physical appearance, build, and prowess.

Perhaps you'll find that your setting doesn't offer enough of a backdrop in which your characters interact. In my Max Austin thrillers, I often have Max travel to several locations to do investigation. I think this leads to an interesting variety of situations and keeps the plot moving.

In other instances, you may find that the storyline of your short story, novella, or novel is failing to convey the ideas you wanted to discuss in your piece. Not that you should be preaching to your readers or trying to convince them of an idea or concept or belief. But your story should raise a question in the minds of your readers that they feel compelled to answer for themselves. If it seems to you that your plot is not bringing about this situation, you may want to rethink the premise, development, and resolution.

In my latest novel, *The ET Murders*, I was well into writing the plot where various organized crime groups were murdering FBI agents and other government officials. The idea was that these criminals would be given certain leeway in exchange for supporting new leadership in the U.S. government. And this leadership would take over power by eliminating other leaders currently in place.

At one point in the novel, I had the FBI lab analyze blood found on a ring belonging to an FBI agent who was attacked and killed in Topeka, Kansas. Then the thought hit me: *What if the blood specimen was found to be something entirely unexpected and unexplainable?* From there, the idea went to the blood being that of an alien, and then to Max Austin finding clues that led to Roswell and Area 51. He investigates the possible reality of UFOs and extraterrestrials on Earth, and he must also determine whether there was a connection with the murders.

I was astounded by the wealth of information about UFOs and aliens that exists and how much of that body of knowledge has been hidden from the public by the military and by government agencies such as the FAA, CIA, and NSA. Is there a reason for not informing civilians about government knowledge of UFOs and aliens? Are we in danger? Can the government do anything to protect us? These are questions I think the book will raise in readers' minds.

So, I advise that as a writer you should remain creative and flexible and willing to take chances with your plot. You'll probably find yourself writing a far more complex, fascinating, and captivating storyline than you originally conceived. Let your characters come alive and have willpower. Consider whether alternate settings might infuse new energy into your story. And be willing to challenge both yourself and your readers by painting your protagonist into darker and tighter corners where he (and you) will have to use all his energy, know-how, and mental prowess to determine a solution to the problems and obstacles you've placed in his path.

Remember that conflict is the key element in fiction. Don't allow your character an easy stroll along a daisy-lined, flat path to reach his goal. Make him work and sweat and bleed and fight anguish, despair, and fear in order to climb the bramble-laden, slippery, mountainous trail you've devised to torture him into fighting for success. Also remember that he's learned a lesson, overcome a fault, and become a better and stronger person from having surmounted the trials and tribulations you've put him through. And yes, you'll have become a more professional and captivating writer by using this process.

Mark Bouton writes mystery and nonfiction books. He worked for the FBI and "nabbed killers, kidnappers, and bank robbers." He also played a key role in solving the Oklahoma City bombing. He uses his experiences to inform his writing. His books move fast, with lots of action, humor, strange characters, and striking plot twists.

He has also written a nonfiction book about how to tell when someone's lying. He has learned to read faces, bodies, and voices to avoid being fooled ever again.

WHY EDIT?

By Maxine Bringenberg

"Words! Words! Words! I'm so sick of words!
I get words all day through; first from him, now from you.
Is that all you blighters can do?"

—From *My Fair Lady*, song "Show Me"

As an editor of books, authors often give me credit for their work reading so well by the time it gets to the publisher. I am always quick to remind them that the book is their "baby"; they gave birth to it. All I do is give it a bath. This response is usually received with humor, but every author knows exactly what I mean when I say it.

When a reader picks up a book, they expect to be entertained, to be swept away to another world where they can escape their own lives for a while. A well-edited — or clean — book allows them to make the journey effortlessly, and to close the book feeling like they were personally involved in the story. However, if there are errors in punctuation, typos, problems with the flow of words, or other editing issues, the reader may feel shortchanged, having been pulled away from the fantasy by the all too real flaws. A good story is still a good story, but editing issues may keep it from being a *great* story.

The irony is that few people will truly notice when a book is flawless, but every reader will notice just a couple of mistakes.

So, what makes a good editor? Obviously, a good grasp of the language (I'll use English as my example) is a must. A doctorate in English is not necessary — nor is remembering your sixth grade lessons on how to diagram a sentence — but knowing how to use nouns, verbs, punctuation, and hundreds of other oft-forgotten rules for the language is mandatory. Perhaps even more important is knowing how to use resources to find answers, because even the best editor will most certainly *not* have them all. Many style manuals exist to instruct writers, editors, and other word users in the use of the English language. In addition, the Internet provides a treasure trove of sources, as do other editors, professionals, friends, and family. Just remember that it's important to check your sources.

In addition, an editor must always be on the watch for factual, spelling and capitalization, continuity, and point of view errors. Again, the Internet is an instant fact-checking source, as well as a great place to check spelling and capitalization, and usually allows the editor to handle the issue rapidly. Continuity issues are a little more difficult, and may require scrolling back and forth within the manuscript, or once again consulting the Internet.

One example would be if a heroine's age is stated early in the book to be twenty-five, but two weeks later in the story she is said to be twenty-eight. This seems to be a small detail, but not changing it would affect the validity of the story.

Another continuity issue might be if a character in a book set in 1965 is using a cell phone. Most people know that cell phones had not been invented yet, and again, this small detail could seriously affect the believability of the story. A good editor would recognize, research, and point out or change these issues.

Point of view, or head hopping from character to character, is also a common issue, but a good editor should be able to spot it and notify the author to correct it.

As I stated before, the author is the one who gives "birth" to the book, but a good editor should take as much pride in "bathing" it as the author did in writing it. What could be more fulfilling than knowing that you're helping to bring a book into the world for readers' enjoyment? An author should always be able to feel that his or her work is important to the editor, because that guarantees the editor will give the book the time and attention it deserves.

Every author knows that promoting his or her work is key in getting it into the hands of readers. An editor worth his salt will take every opportunity to assist in promoting the work, whether by word of mouth, social media, or other avenues.

Many editors work or contract for more than one publishing company at a time, and take on several projects at once. There is nothing wrong with this, unless the editor gets so bogged down with work that she can't provide good services for any of her authors or publishers. A good editor can recognize his or her own limitations, and not take on more projects than he or she can realistically handle. If an author feels that his work is not being handled professionally, he should contact the person to whom the editor reports to request intervention.

An editor's primary purpose is to make sure that the author's work is published in a clean, error-free format. Many factors can affect the editing process, and the author, the editor, and at times the publisher should work together to make sure these factors have positive influences on the final manuscript.

1. All people involved in the writing, editing, and publishing process are a team, and must work together with the same goal in mind...to publish the best work possible.
2. An author must not take editing notes and changes personally. While it can be difficult to see another person change something that you labored over, try to remember that the editor is not attacking the work, but making improvements to help the book sell when it is published.
3. An editor must remember that the manuscript they are editing is the brainchild of another person, and that person...the author...should be given the respect, consideration, and editorial input capabilities that they rightfully deserve.
4. While an editor is usually considered the so-called "expert" on the written word, no one is infallible, so the author's wishes should be considered when a change is questioned. Hopefully, the team approach will lead to a resolution that both parties can embrace.
5. An author should always feel free to discuss issues or questions they have about the editing process with the editor. If you, as the author, have a specific reason for writing something that the editor has changed, speak up and let the editor know. Communication, whether it is via email, text messages, or phone contact, is absolutely key to a successful author/editor relationship.

6. If the author has confidence in their editor and knows that their work will be treated professionally, their creativity may be enhanced and allowed to flow more freely.
7. Most authors appreciate a good editor. Many authors go into a "zone" when they write, and depend on the editor to keep them on track and to ensure the quality of the final draft.
8. On occasion, disputes will arise between authors and editors, usually relating to the style of editing. If this occurs, once again remember the ultimate goal and try to arrive at a mutually agreeable solution. When necessary, consult another person who is in a position to make the decision and resolve the dispute.
9. The written word is one of the most valuable things the world has ever possessed.

Anyone can write down words to a story, but only those who are blessed with the author's muse can write in such a way that the world will sit up and take notice. Editors are equally blessed to be able to help these gifted individuals share their stories with the world.

Maxine Horton Bringenberg was raised in the mountains of northeastern Kentucky, in a little town on the Ohio River, and calls herself a "river rat." Life has allowed her to live in many locations, including Atlanta and Florida's Gulf Coast, but she currently resides in a suburb of Columbus, Ohio with her husband, two grown children, and four cats. Much of her adult life has been spent working with adults with special needs, and also in the health care field. But since childhood, Maxine has had a love of the written word, and a few years ago was delighted to be given the opportunity to edit mostly fictional books. While she has not yet published a book of her own, the authors she works with now are a constant source of inspiration, and she hopes to find her muse soon.

ON MY EXPERIENCE IN TEACHING AND WRITING

John Emil Augustine

Most high schools have done a pretty good job of making people groan when the words "English" and "Class" are uttered in the same breath. How much time did we all spend in those classes? I understood what most students (the good and the not-so-good ones) were thinking and feeling when getting basically the same thing right out of the shoot in college. It was a real "you gotta be kidding me" moment. After all, hadn't they suffered enough in high school?

But the beauty of teaching college English was that I was able to get into some of the interesting stuff about the language and the creative process that apparently no one had ever gotten to in high school. My class was a bit of an eye-opener for students and I had a heck of a lot of fun. I was neither a grammar Nazi nor a fine-toothed editor, though I could be both when appropriate.

I was far more attuned to the creative process … that thing that gets stomped out of most people by teachers. The creative process is what writes proposals and emails and resumes and copy for radio and letters of intent and advertisements for your business … everything, really. Without the ability to utilize your creativity, you sit there staring at a blank paper or computer monitor and become pissed off because you know you can't do it. How do you know you can't do it? In many, many cases it's because of crappy experiences with crappy grading systems.

Unfortunately, what we rarely if ever were graded on in school was the first draft: the horrible version of the eventual product. *And it's the most important thing you will do when writing anything.* Nobody seemed to tell us that. So much attention was given to what a paper looked like in the end that we began to believe that every word needed to come out "right" or we were just wasting our time. Then when at first we could not get it to look "right" (whatever that means), we would become frustrated, and BOOM! Suddenly what we were doing was writing something horrible and we would give up. That's most people's creative process.

A true creative process is just that: a process. A writer must process his or her thoughts and feelings, and it can be difficult. Perhaps I should write that it can't *not* be difficult. A process should not *only* be difficult, however. We process to learn. And we clarify the process in order to turn around and share what we've learned. At some point the process will be enlightening. That exchange, that communication was something I tried to emphasize to my students.

So what I did as a teacher was to say forget the finished product. That is secondary, if that, because if you have nothing to work with in the first place, you will end up with nothing. Your first ideas, dumb as they may be, are the most important part of creating anything. I would say jot them down — all of them. Map them, list them, web them, write them — use whatever technique from whatever textbook you want. It is all the same idea — get the good and the bad stuff on the page. Once a student got as much as he or she could onto the paper, we could make the rest happen in class together. But we needed something to work with in the first place.

I would say, "Write it on a napkin or a cereal box and turn that in." For some reason, students loved that idea: the first draft could look like crap and still be worth something in my class. I really didn't care what the draft looked like at first read, as long as it was something. The first draft, in any condition, was half the paper's grade. That's pretty good encouragement when you've already got 50/100 just for writing something … anything.

I actually was encouraging crap. It was often a very new concept. You can see why the so-called problem students did well in my class! Even a crappy writer can turn in crap. In fact, with most of my students, they felt that their specialty was, in fact, crap. In my class, we could work with crap. After all, we've all got to start somewhere. Starting with something awful meant only that we were starting, and that was at least half the battle. I was amazed how many people didn't understand that concept prior to the class. It was like a life jacket for someone who was drowning in a perception of his or her own awful writing ability. Half your grade was based on doing something awful. Talk about good news for someone used to barely getting Ds in writing. Heck, it was good news for someone who was used to getting A's.

Then, of course, the bad news would come, but in a slightly new light. Quite simply, each paper would have a version of this written on it: "Here's how many more points you would get if you called this your final draft and here's what to do to get more points" — or — "Here is where the draft you just turned in falls on the continuum between the 50 points you have now and the 100 points that will get you an A+." A paper could, for example, score about 60/100 if turned in again as it was and someone could walk away with a D on the paper.

That was a pretty normal occurrence, a rough draft equaling 60/100 points were it turned in as a final draft. Once in a while someone would take me up on the 60/100 on their paper, but usually students would look at my comments and say, "This is all I need to do to get an A!?!" Once you have something to work with, the editing is so much more achievable. Sometimes the editing is hard and sometimes it is easy, but if you do it in steps, a little at a time, it really isn't the perplexity that we've been led to believe. It's just like any other process. You do it until you are satisfied and until you think your audience is going to understand it. I was just there to help at that point.

Everything needed to be modeled several ways several times and I did that for them, writing along with them during my own exercises. They needed to see it as many ways and times as it took to get comfortable with the process, and they needed to see it from me as well as their peers. Trying and trying again was integral to the class. Once students saw and began to try the creative and the editing processes, the whole thing turned into small steps that were tolerable and knowable.

There was no limit on drafts. If someone turned in draft #2 and was satisfied with 70/100, so be it. If someone turned in draft #8 and still wasn't satisfied with 98/100, a draft #9 was fine with me. Complete control of their own destiny with lots of help or no help if someone didn't want it — everything was up to the student. I set the standard and they could take it or leave it knowing they had the control and the help.

That is communication. That's how you keep people interested and learning even though they initially don't want to be there. The quality is not compromised and neither is the students' integrity.

I loved seeing people who were adamantly against writing turn completely around and try. I marveled at my students as they did. The excitement was electric and I went home charged up more times than not. Now I encourage everyone to try writing: blogs, travelogues, emails to relatives, whatever. Find someone who inspires your writing — an author, a teacher, a blog show host — and soak it in. Then turn around and try it. For me, it has been an incredibly rewarding pastime: my way to sort through all kinds of bullshit I am hanging onto, to get it out of the way, and to live again.

We all need something that helps us process our life, and writing can be it. I still have students who get in touch and let me know they are still writing… without groaning! Whether I was the one who opened eyes or not isn't really important. The importance was in their trying. After having tried, the process and the result can be quite enlightening and exciting; in my case, extremely liberating. After all, as I used to tell my students, each of us *has* suffered enough.

John Emil Augustine is an author at Master Koda Select Publishing. He toured in his twenties and early thirties with local and national acts; writing, arranging, and performing on the road with well-known Jazz, Blues, Gospel, Reggae, Post Funk, Prog Rock, and Folk Rock groups. John has also been a landscaper, mail carrier, English professor, and forklift operator. He currently lives in Minneapolis, MN with his wife and four boys.

Learn more about him by visiting these websites: http://masterkodaselectpublishing.com and http://www.johnemilaugustine.com

10 BLOCKBUSTING CURES FOR WRITER'S BLOCK

By Faith McDonald and David McDonald

For any writer suffering from "writer's block" here are ten of our own tried and true cures:

First: Quit thinking of writing as a purely creative action. It is a job, and as such, it must be performed daily. When we think of it as a job, we remove permission to wait upon the creative juices to flow. We understand that writing is a constant ability resident within us that we can call upon when it is needed, and that is daily. Allowing this change of perspective will trigger psychological changes within you, which will cause ideas to flow.

Second: Don't wait to *feel* good or to "like writing" in order to write. Be disciplined by being your own master over how you feel. Don't buy into the so-called "artist's prerogative" to be emotionally unstable — as if we need emotionally instability in order to be creative. Artists who were historically defined this way were also destroyed this way. Be professional and not flaky.

Third: Think your characters through before you sit down to write. Good stories come from good characters. Develop your characters well and the story will naturally and logically ensue from their interactive behaviors. See the story in your heart and mind before you write it. This will save you from staring at a blank screen when you could be looking over a serene lake as your characters come to life in your mind's eye.

Fourth: Don't be afraid to let your characters live and lead you through the story. In other words, develop them well and they will write the story for you. Make sure your characters have attributes with which others can relate and aspire. Several of these qualities are flaws, uniqueness, ambitions, dreams, inner conflicts, unresolved issues, fixations and hopes of resolving all these.

Fifth: I'm sure that you've heard the admonition to "write about what you know." Without doubt, this is good advice, but inherent in this axiom is the implication that productive writers must know a lot about many things. It follows then that writers must also be readers who are excited about learning and curious about ideas and subject matter from various fields other than those with which they are comfortably familiar.

Sixth: There are many aspects to writing that may be rotated to fit the constraints of the day. For example, let's say that your not *feeling* very inspired and no act of discipline can make the ideas come. No problem! It's a great day to proofread your work by checking your grammar, plot lines, consistency, facts or you can even study other reading material. On the other hand, if you're feeling creative and the juices are flowing, then don't hinder the creation of ideas by correcting run-on sentences. Or, say you only have a little time to work on a certain day. That's a good day to just read your work as though it hadn't been written by you. What seemed like an unproductive day suddenly becomes a golden opportunity to acquire a deeper degree of objectivity to your writing.

Seven: Avoid copying styles of other authors by reading a wide array of material from various sources. This diversity of input will broaden your scope of understanding, which in turn will open your mind to creative options that otherwise might have remained hidden. You will find your own, unique voice hidden within the voices of many. It is exciting to find one's own unique writing voice, and excitement about writing is a guaranteed block-busting mechanism.

Eight: Write to sell. If you keep in mind that you are writing in order to sell your work, then all that you write will have the expectations of your target audience in mind. You'll constantly be aware of the fact that you must keep the reader's attention and engage him or her in the story on many different levels. Remember, the story — or whatever you are writing — is *by* you, but not *for* you. Publishers aren't interested in an author's vain attempt of self-expression or healing. Writing is a business, and books must be sold to stay in business. So, unless you can bridge the gap between self-expression and the ability of others to relate and benefit from your work, then your work's appeal shall remain confined to you alone.

Nine: If you become stuck in a place in your work, then it is definitely time to stop writing and start reading what you have written. Go to the beginning of your work and begin reading it as if it was the first time though. This will refresh and established the plot lines in your mind and will often inspire new plot twist possibilities that oftentimes wind up turning a good work into an absolute masterpiece.

Ten: Conceivably, there is no end to the number of proofreads, rewrites, revisions, editing and polishing that a written work must go through to be its best and, yet, at some point you must declare your work finished. It's not writer's block when we refuse to submit our finished work to the publisher. That's just fear of a damaged ego. Fact: your work will be rejected many times before it is accepted. Writers must develop mental toughness and faith in their work if they are to endure these cold refusals. Be willing to accept constructive criticism and allow it to change how you write so that what was once coldly rejected becomes something warmly accepted. Conversely, don't allow your work to be changed when you know it's right the way it is written. In this case, submit it to other publishers.

Writing is work and, yes, it is even hard work. That, however, doesn't mean we writers can't enjoy what we do. In fact, since we humans tend to do what we enjoy and avoid that which we do not, then necessity dictates that we discover ways of enjoying all the processes of writing if, that is, we hope to continue to share our ideas with the world.

NO, I WON'T USE AN E-READER

by Mark Rubenstein

Let me begin by saying I *love* books, whether electronic or paper. I'll read on my Kindle or a "regular" book. Frankly, I'll read on whatever's available. I just love reading and being transported to another world beyond my own. It's pleasurable to share the domain the writer has created. It's a realm to which I bring my own thoughts, feelings, fantasies and experiences, all of which, no doubt, color my reading experience. It's the *experience* of taking in the writer's creation that's so meaningful, not the medium by which it's delivered.

I've heard many people refuse to *consider* using an e-reader. There seems to be an impenetrable wall of resistance to even the notion of using a reading device. It's the usual mantra about loving the "feel" or "smell" of paper, or the pleasure derived from holding a *real* book in hand. Or perhaps it's the physical act of turning pages, or the heft of the book itself.

I, too, love the sensory elements of reading a paper book, but that hasn't precluded me from using an e-reader. After all, one reading medium doesn't rule out the other.

Why do some people refuse — absolutely reject — the idea?

It's not that they're knuckle-draggers or technophobes because they often have smart phones, iPods, computers and Skype. And, I've noticed the repudiation of e-readers isn't limited to older people. I know plenty of people under forty who, despite being completely comfortable with the technology of our times, want absolutely nothing to do with reading devices.

So, what exactly causes them to spurn this one technology?

I've thought about it as a psychiatrist, writer and avid reader. Maybe it's because reading is something cultivated over the course of a lifetime, often beginning in childhood. Many book-lovers were read to as children — by a parent, babysitter, or some other adult. It was, for most of us, a very special thing.

"Read me a story" is something most of us can remember asking, if we think back to our earliest formative years. "Being read to" is an experience that becomes embedded in our psyches as a distinct and unique childhood pleasure. It's loaded with meaning, and is suffused with memories of nestling on Mommy's or Daddy's lap; the look of the book with its bright, colorful illustrations; or the feel of the paper while we helped turn the pages. The physical book itself became the symbol housing the powerful emotional satisfaction of having parental attention bestowed upon us with all its attendant meanings.

The book encapsulated a deep sense of pleasure, safety, wonder, satisfaction, and above all, love. These early experiences, and their residue, linger with us, and can have enormous emotional resonance.

On a pre-conscious level, perhaps some of us refuse to even *try* an e-reader because our minds view it as a renunciation of one of life's earliest pleasures.

It's merely my theory, but when I reflect upon how readily other technologies are embraced, none of them carry the primal significance of a "book in the hand."

Mark Rubinstein was born in Brooklyn, New York. He graduated from New York University with a degree in business administration. He then served in the army and ended up as a field medic tending to paratroopers of the 82nd Airborne Division. He was so taken with these experiences that after his discharge, he re-entered NYU as a premed student. He entered medical school at the State University of New York's Downstate Medical Center. As a medical student, he developed an interest in psychiatry, discovering in that specialty the same thing he realized in reading fiction: every patient has a compelling story to tell. He became a board-certified psychiatrist practicing in New York City.

In addition to running his private practice he developed an interest in forensic psychiatry because the drama and conflict of the cases and courtrooms tapped into his personality style. He also taught psychiatric residents, interns, psychologists, and social workers at New York Presbyterian Hospital and became a clinical assistant professor at Cornell University's medical school.

Before turning to fiction, Rubinstein coauthored five medical self-help books: *The First Encounter: The Beginnings in Psychotherapy*, *The Complete Book of Cosmetic Facial Surgery*, *New Choices: the Latest Options in Treating Breast Cancer*, *Heartplan: A Complete Program for Total Fitness of Heart & Mind*, and *The Growing Years: A Guide to Your Child's Emotional Development from Birth to Adolescence.*

Rubinstein lives in Connecticut with his wife and as many dogs as she will allow in the house. He still practices psychiatry and is busily writing more novels. *Mad Dog House*, his first novel, was named a Finalist for the 2012 ForeWord Reviews Book of the Year Award (Thriller & Suspense). His second novel, *Love Gone Mad*, coming out this September, is available for preorder through Mark's website, www.MarkRubinstein-Author.com

WRITING IN A MIRROR

By Brian M. Hayden

I do not know why I write the things I write. I do not know if any writer truly understands the foundation or inspiration for what they write. Ok, sometimes we do, but sometimes, a guy just wants to write stuff that seems impossible. Sometimes a guy wants to write things to test themselves, and sometimes…just sometimes on that rare occasion, a guy just wants to write a story about writing a story.

I was thinking about writing a story about thinking about writing a story. How cool would that be if I could actually pull something like that off? I was not sure how to begin. Would I begin by writing down my thoughts? Then slowly define and expound on them? Or, would it be better to just jump right in and write about wanting to write. I don't know. Let me think about it for a moment.

(a moment later)

So I think what I have decided to do is just jump right into a story. My story is tentatively called, Writing the Fable or… WTF I have not decided yet.

I think that the most difficult part of this exercise is writing in coherent thoughts whilst (I always wanted to say that) not appearing to be or actually being random and scattered. You know what I mean? Some authors tend to jump on their bandwagon and just ramble about nothing. That makes me crazy, especially when I can see a great story just under the surface waiting to come out.

So, I am here at my desk, thinking, thinking, thinking … and then it occurs to me. If I actually write a story, the first sentence in the first paragraph will have become incorrect, for the moment I stop thinking about writing a story and actually write a story, the jig is up.

I ponder writing about an old couple. They have been together for a very long time. In fact, they are basking in the glow of their 60th wedding anniversary and are still on vacation in New York City. New York City, specifically Brooklyn, holds a very dear place in both of their hearts, because it was there that the two met.

But then reality set in and I began to have a conversation with myself. I did not recall if the conversation was in my head or out loud, but I am certain it was interesting. I wonder, How far can I take this concept? *It is too crazy. It is too difficult to figure out.* How can I proceed with my protagonist? *Wait. If there is more than one main character, is there a plural form of the word "protagonist?" I will leave that to the editors. For now, I will try to figure out a storyline.*

How did they meet? That may be the right way to begin the story. Talk about each person and tell the reader how they met. Maybe I could begin with the guy. Oh, let me begin by introducing them to you.

First, the guy. His name is Bartholomew. As you may surmise, with a name like that, he comes from money. Lots of money. He wants for nothing his entire life, except for one thing. He has wanted to experience the world as every other regular person experiences it. He rarely gets that opportunity but one day when he was barely 18 years old, Bartholomew slipped out of the large house and headed for a park. He left Manhattan, which was his home, took the subway to Brooklyn and walked the streets. Enjoying the differences, soaking up the ambience, he finds his way to 7th Avenue.

Wonderful shops and cafes line most of 7th Avenue as he heads west from Flatbush Avenue. Finally getting to 11th Street, he decides to make a left and head up the sloped street. Two blocks up, as he reaches 9th Avenue, and he sees what was yearned for by his heart. A park. It was Prospect Park and there were wonderful hot dog vendors and others plying their wares. Crossing 9th Avenue, Bartholomew wore a huge grin on his face, and the feel of satisfaction deep within his soul — he walks straight for the hot dogs.

Our lady, Doris, is a very different character. She is a born and bred 17-year-old Brooklyn girl, coming from the area where Ditmas and Coney Island Avenue intersect. For the time, it was a very blue collar, but respectable, neighborhood. The "F" train stopped just a couple of blocks from her home, so Central Park was very close, and from her earliest year Central Park quickly became a favorite adventure for her and her friends.

Doris just loved Central Park, but on this cold and windy day, she decided to shorten her trip and go to Prospect Park. The short journey took her to the 9th Street Station, where Prospect Park was only steps away.

Now comes the hard part. How can I transition from both characters, each in their own worlds, to finding each other in a fun, or romantic way? Let me think about this for a minute.

Thinking... Thinking... What do you think about doing it this way?

So both Doris and Bartholomew were walking around the Prospect Park area. It was a chilly fall day, and the wind blew hard, knocking off the remainder of the golden and brown leaves and stacking them neatly on the edges of curbs. Even the birds hid from the bitter cold wind.

There is an area where 11th Street meets 9th Avenue, where the grand entrance into the park is located. Often times, hot dog vendors would be available, and in the summer, cotton candy and ice cream, too. Today, as winter was taking aim on the park, there was the hot dog man accompanied by a coffee and hot chocolate cart and a guy roasting chestnuts. The smells from the trio of vendors was warm and inviting. People lingered within nostril's range, and it was at this point that the two of them first locked eyes.

Is that the right way for them to meet, I wonder? What if there could be a more "meet cute" way of getting them together. Let me think a moment.

Several moments later...

No. I think that way is fine. Wait. No. How about this?

Bartholomew had just ordered a hot dog loaded with the typical New York accouterments: mustard, sauerkraut and onions. The sauerkraut was the kind that makes your face squeeze closed when the acidity of the vinegar first touches your tongue. The sauerkraut had this strange sour-sweet rust colored sauce blended into it and the hot dog vendor piled the sour-sweet vegetable on the dog, all nestled in the warm, steamed bun. Then he added chopped onions, sprinkling them on the top. A slice of sour — not dill — pickle accompanied the hot dog.

Bartholomew was sitting on the edge of the rock wall that lined the entrance to the park and sculpted the flowerbeds that are now at rest. His steaming coffee was sitting patiently by his side.

Eating hot dogs in the park is a passion for many New Yorkers. It was for Bartholomew on those rare occasions when he can escape from the life that traps him. With hardly a care in the world, he held his hot dog, and at least for now, all in the world was well.

As he began eating his masterpiece, the juice from the sauerkraut fell slowly from his mouth to his chin. There were small pieces of half masticated onion and bright yellow mustard sitting on the side of his mouth, waiting patiently to be caught by his tongue and brought into his mouth for their final journey. That was okay, though. Making a mess was just part of the deal. Besides, he was by himself, and as anyone who knows New Yorkers can attest, New Yorkers really do not care what other people think, that is unless that other person is someone of the opposite sex.

I could bring Doris in at this point. She could have a playful smile on her face and a hand full of napkins.

She quietly approaches Bartholomew. Sitting next to him with her steaming cup of hot chocolate, she offers our guy a napkin, pointing at his chin and grinning. He cleans his chin. Then she points at the side of his mouth and his cheek. He is embarrassed. She is beaming. He cleans himself up and makes the introductions.

Then I wonder, What do I do with them now? *I cannot think of anything original or novel to do with them. Of course the usual stuff comes to mind. Falling in love, falling out of love and then after time finding each other again and falling back in love. Too much falling for my taste. Too dangerous. No, there must be something original. But what? Let me think.*

Thinking. Patience please. Brilliance does not happen quickly.

Later that afternoon, I returned to my computer and the task at hand. Let's see... What to write? ... hmmm, hum. What to write? I HAVE IT!

Well, actually it is the next morning, and I still do not have a good way for the new couple to proceed. Maybe I could start simply with introductions. After all, she did point out the mess on his face. Perhaps it could go like this:

He cleans himself, a bit embarrassed, he summons up his courage and says "Thank you. My name is Bartholomew." He then extends his hand in the obligatory gesture.

Doris, too, extended her hand to meet his. As they clasped hands, she said, "Hello Bartholomew. My name is Doris."

Before she could get another word out, he interrupts, "A pleasure to meet you, Doris", he says while starring at her pretty eyes.

He is wondering if there are still some remnants of his hot dog feast on his face, so as he says Doris, it comes out with a bit of a tremble. Then silence. Both staring into the others eyes, mesmerized and silent. Doris felt her heart pounding and Bartholomew, well let's just say he was very happy.

I think after the introductions, I will have them go for a walk through the park.

Slow, gliding steps see them through the beautiful barren tree-scapes. They talk about lots of stuff. They talked about everything and before they knew it, the day was out and they were holding hands.

I do not dare take this experiment any further. I think that the notion of writing about writing is intriguing, but ridiculous. Consequently, I am going to stop. Besides, you know how the story will end. They fall in love, and live happily ever after. Of course, there is the obligatory drama. Fights with the family, the occasional indiscretion — for which he forgives her. See, you instantly thought it was he. Ha! Then, sixty years of marriage brings them both back to the intersection of 9th avenue and 11th street in Brooklyn. In the last paragraph, they are standing on the corner, looking across the street as they did all of those years ago. They walk to the entrance of the park, where the hot dog cart was, and all of those savory toppings. The coffee and hot chocolate guy as well as the roasted chestnut guy are all present on this cold winter day, and the smell of the trio of vendors filled the air.

Brian M. Hayden was born in Chicago, Illinois in 1954 into a middle class, blue collar Jewish family. He and his family moved to the suburbs of Los Angeles, California in 1961. He is a second-generation born American son of Austrian and English grandparents on his father's side and Polish and Russian grandparents on his mother's side. Hayden enlisted in the Air Force in 1972 and finally was medically discharged July 1990. Up until now, his writing had been limited to writing works of non-fiction. He has written a management book, several scripts for educational videos and two memoirs. He is actually in the midst of writing a third. He married a wonderful girl, Denise in August of 1974, and is happy to announce they are still very much in love, and happily married after more than 38 years. They have two children. Joseph is married and provided them with three absolutely wonderful grandsons. Their daughter Angela is also married and provided an addition three very special step grandsons. They currently reside in San Antonio, Texas.

Find Brian on Facebook, visit his website at www.BrianHayden.net/, his blog at http://brianhayden.net/bog/, his Amazon page and find him on LinkedIn.

WHERE ARE THEY NOW?

By Donald Riggio

The decade between the years 1954 and 1964 is often referred to as, *the Golden age of rock and roll.* Fifty-four saw the first documented use of the term *rock n' roll,* in promoting a show radio disc jockey Alan Freed put on at St. Nicholas Arena in New York City. Also in '54, the songs, "Shake, Rattle and Roll," and "Rock Around the Clock," were popularized by Bill Haley and His Comets. Elvis Presley made his first commercial records at Sam Phillips Sun Record Studios in Memphis, Tennessee. And, the vocal groups the Chords (an African-American group), and the Crew-Cuts (a white group) released the same song, "Sh-Boom," which the Crew-Cuts took to #1 on the national charts, despite the fact the Chord's version came out first.

Whether you called it Doo-Wop or street corner music, the lush, harmonic sounds emanating from the streets, subway stations, tenement hallways, or high school restrooms dominated the urban landscape of every major city coast to coast. Groups of teenage boys and girls were discovered by the score by independent record labels that sprung up seemingly overnight. They signed contracts with managers and companies who coached, packaged and promoted them and their music. Some were only one-hit wonders, whose careers flashed like rice paper set to flame and were then gone, but others enjoyed great success and saw their careers flourish.

By 1964, Alan Freed had been convicted of tax evasion for taking money for playing certain songs on the radio. A worldwide explosion took place when the British Invasion of music groups and performers came ashore in a virtual tsunami of talent spearheaded by the Beatles from Liverpool, England. Their appearances on the Ed Sullivan Show sent female fans in droves to record stores to purchase their 45's and LP's, and male fans to music stores to buy guitars and learn how to play.

They were followed in quick succession by artists like The Rolling Stones, The Dave Clark Five, Petula Clark and countless others. Some American acts never recovered while other slipped into a veritable four-year hiatus, to return with the Oldies Revival Era in 1969. In some cases they even surpass their former glory, as they continued on through the subsequent decades.

Their fans, now known as "baby boomers," treasure the memories those artists and songs bring to our consciousness and avidly follow them via "oldies" radio stations, either on the AM or FM air-waves or on social networking pages like Facebook on the Internet.

Sadly, a good number of the artists are no longer with us and we lose the talents of others almost every day. Recording legends like Johnny Maestro who fronted the Crests in the late fifties and then the Brooklyn Bridge until his passing in 2010, along with

Earl "Speedoo" Carroll of the Cadillacs who left us in 2012, have gone on to their eternal rewards.

Other Rock and Roll stars battle through debilitating illness but continue to perform if and when they can. Aretha Franklin has recently cancelled shows because of an undisclosed illness. Just last year, Bobby Rydell underwent double organ transplant surgery to replace his liver and kidneys, and is already back out on the road.

The good news is that there is still plenty of that "old time Rock and Roll," out there for us to enjoy. Stars that continue to fill big venues include, Dion, Mary Wilson, formerly of the Supremes who tour worldwide, as do the Beach Boys, Frankie Valli and the Four Seasons, Little Anthony and the Imperials, Smokey Robinson and Neil Sedaka. Chubby Checker has fans young and old doing "The Twist," and all of its offshoots to the glee of Chiropractors everywhere.

Promoters across the country put together road show concerts like the ones we attended as kids at The Brooklyn Fox, The Paramount, and The Apollo theaters. They provide a full evening of entertainment with a list of acts.

Charlie Thomas' Drifters take us "Up on the Roof," and "Under the Boardwalk," while Terry Johnson's Flamingos enchant us with, "I Only Have Eyes for You." Herb Cox and the Cleftones, provide so many "Sentimental Reasons." Larry Chance and the Earls continue to urge us to "Remember Then."

John Kuse and the Excellents still love their "Coney Island Baby," while Jimmy Gallagher and the Passions will probably never get over "Gloria." Jimmy Beaumont and the Skyliners, features the lilting voice of a female soprano in the classic, "Since I Don't have You," as do the Demensions with, "Over the Rainbow."

Girl groups like, The Chantels, Chiffons, Crystals, Shirelles, Martha and the Vandellas and Angels share stages with the likes of, Jay Siegel's Tokens singing their mega-hit, "The Lion Sleeps Tonight," along with the Jive Five, Dubs, and Capris.

Male and female solo artists abound. Lloyd Price continues to warn us of that bad man, "Stagger Lee." Gene Chandler in top hat, tails and cane struts rock and roll royalty center stage as, "The Duke of Earl." The *Iceman* Jerry Butler captivates audiences with his *belly-rubbing* classic, "For Your Precious Love." Kathy Young, still sees, "A Thousand Stars in the Sky," while Leslie Gore reminds us that, "It's My Party," and "You Don't Own me."

And, as he has done since 1992, Kenny Vance (a founding member of Jay and the Americans) still has his group, the Planotones, "Looking for an Echo."

Someone once said, "Rock and Roll will never die…it will always be." There's no denying that fact. It stands, along with Jazz and Rhythm and Blues, as a truly American art form.

Many of the performers included in this article have websites where you can easily find their performance schedules and contact information. Do yourself a favor and get out and see a show that features the greatest music of all time, the music of the 50's and 60's. Can't get to a concert? No problem, www.youtube.com offers literally thousands of songs by many great artists guaranteed to bring back happy memories.

Donald Riggio was born and raised in the Bronx, New York and has had a deep and enduring love of rock and roll music since he was a boy. His love of writing is equally enduring as is illustrated in his success as a short story and technical writer over the years.

He combined his two passions with the publication of his first novel, *Seven-Inch Vinyl: A Rock and Roll Novel*, in 2011. That book became a #1 Kindle Best Seller in the music category as did the sequel, *Beyond Vinyl: The Rock and Roll Saga Continues* published in 2012.

He also hosts a successful Facebook page, where he and his 3,500+ friends discuss, post pictures, rock and roll song links and information 24/7. He invites everyone to join him.

Mr. Riggio lives in Las Vegas, Nevada, where he is currently writing the third book in his trilogy, When Gold Turns to Gray.

FEATURED AUTHORS

BLACKBERRY SUMMER

Author: RaeAnne Thayne
Series: Hope's Crossing #1
Page count: 414
ISBN: 978-1611733471
Formats: Large Print, Paperback, ebook

A Book-of-the-Month, Rhapsody and Doubleday Bookclub alternate selection!

Find the author: www.RaeanneThayne.com

REVIEW BY FRAN LEWIS

Hope's Crossing is a small close-knit town in Colorado, where everyone seems concerned about his or her fellow residents. Claire Bradford's life, however, has been turned upside down when her husband and high school love, Jeff, decides to leave her for another woman — his secretary, Holly. *Imagine living in the same town with your ex-husband and his new wife.* Although Holly is totally materialistic, and adores shopping and showing off her latest acquisitions, she is not the typical second wife. She has bonded with Claire's two children, and is trying to befriend Claire, too.

The novel opens with a robbery. String Fever, Claire's business, where she creates original pieces of jewelry and accessories and teaches women how to bead, has been ransacked and robbed. A beautiful wedding gown she is supposed to bead has been ripped to shreds. *Imagine walking into your business in the morning and seeing the devastation.* Why would anyone want to hurt her by robbing her store?

Life does not always go the way you want it to, and Claire is about to face more challenges than she expects, including the fact that Riley McKnight, the younger brother of her long-time friend who's had a crush on her for years, has come back to town and is now the new police chief.

In the middle of all of these robberies, someone seems to be helping those in need. They call the unknown benefactor the Angel of Hope. The "angel" gives people money or pays their bills, all anonymously.

Riley pursues the teenaged robbery suspect, who is also the mayor's son, on a slick, snowy road. The dangerous road conditions cause him to eventually stop his pursuit of the pickup, but the driver of the truck speeds up, goes over the divider, and causes an accident that will rock Hope Crossing community. Riley's niece is killed in the accident, and Claire and several others are injured. Riley feels guilty, and blames himself for the accident because he was pursuing the suspects who caused the accidents.

As a result of the accident and his help afterward, Riley and Claire renew their friendship. Riley also becomes close with Claire's son, Owen. Meanwhile, the townspeople try to come to terms with the loss of one life and the rehabilitation of another. It is heartwarming that the kids in this story relate well to adults and adjust so well to what life throws at them. The author brings to light what happens when divorce does not become ugly and those involved can act like adults.

Riley and Claire's budding romance changes as her mother tries to create a rift between them for her own reasons. There is added tension because there are those who feel Riley is the wrong man for police chief. Then, Claire decides to do something to help bring the town together in order to honor Riley's niece's memory, but Riley objects, saying she's downplaying the gravity of her death. As Claire's mother continues to be outspoken about her feelings about Riley, Claire begins to doubt her own feelings, yet defends him to the hilt as a friend. She's confused when he backs off romantically.

This is a story about loyalty, trust, betrayal, companionship, helping, family values, and one town that has its arms wide open to welcome those who decide to call it home.

As the story draws to a close the author leaves us with many unanswered questions. What was the real cause of the accident? What really happened? What will happen to Claire and Riley? Who is the Angel of Hope?

This was one great novel that was filled with great characters, romance, love and understanding. This is an author whose work I will definitely continue to read. Instead of stars, I will give this book: FIVE BEAUTIFUL BEADED BRACELETS FROM STRING FEVER AND FIVE BLACKBERRIES.

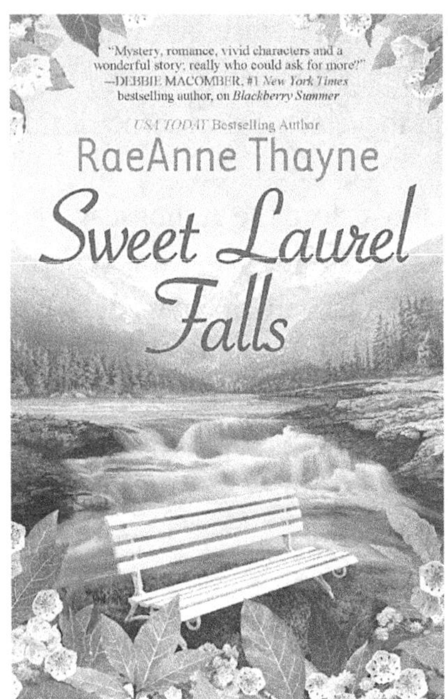

SWEET LAUREL FALLS

Author: RaeAnne Thayne
Series: Hope's Crossing #3
Page count: 384
ISBN: 978-0373776702
Formats: Large Print, Paperback, ebook
Find the author: www.RaeanneThayne.com

REVIEW BY FRAN LEWIS

Maura McKnight-Parker lost her youngest daughter to a drunk-driving accident and her older daughter is away at college. She's been dealing with her loss and trying to cope with life. She's set up the Christmas book club in her bookstore and is excited about it.

Surprises come when you least expect them, and some of them you might want to live without. Maura McKnight never expects that her ex, Jackson Lange, and her older daughter, Sage, will meet and discover their link to each other. Neither of them is happy with Maura when the secret is revealed.

When he left twenty years ago, Jackson Lange never turned back, never gave Maura a second thought. He lived his own life and became a successful architect. He never knew that Sage was his daughter; he didn't even know Maura was pregnant when he left because Maura kept it a secret. So, what drew him back to Hope's Crossing, and what will cause him to stay?

Things start to heat up between Maura and Jackson, and old feelings return, tempers flare, and they find they must come to some kind of truce. Sage, accepts his presence, and is anxious and thrilled to have Jack in her life. But, what about her mother? What about the people in the town and their reaction to Jack?

In addition, Harry Lange, Jackson's cantankerous, difficult, and impossible to get along with father, is one of the wealthiest men in town and seems to have his hand on the pulse of the economy.

Not wanting to lose any more time with his daughter, Jack considers moving to Hope's Crossing, opening an office, and hiring his daughter to work for him, giving her a coveted internship in architecture.

As things progress, it becomes apparent that the feelings between Maura and Jackson are still there, but Maura's just coming out of a relationship with a man named Chris. Will she reconnect with her first love? Maura learns that Jackson never received the messages when she called, which explains why he never returned her calls.

Will they decide that the second time around just might make it right? But sometimes connections are made even when you least expect them to be. The father who has just entered his daughter's life is more perceptive than Maura thinks.

Concerned about what might be causing Sage to become so tired and pale, both Jack and Maura have different thoughts. When expressing his concerns to Maura and what he thinks might be the cause of Sage's tiredness and lethargic behavior, Maura defends her daughter but agrees to seek medical help for her. When the truth comes out and Sage tells them the problem, they band together to help her. What will Maura and Jack do about the secret that Sage has finally revealed?

As Harry attempts to put out an olive branch to his son, Jackson, Sage learns something that might change it all. Secrets, betrayals, lies, and hidden feelings are primary in the final chapters of this outstanding novel. Learning what Sage will do with her problem, dealing with telling the truth and facing the world, and learning something about the Angel of Hope, all work to make things take an interesting turn for everyone.

Can everyone put the past behind them and realize that people can change? Can they learn the true meaning of forgiveness and embrace a new life? This story has an ending that only author RaeAnne Thayne could create, and a family whose lives will never be the same.

Hope's Crossing, the name alone brings you warmth, love, and makes you smile. The special butterflies in the memorial scene (you must read the book to learn the details) reminded me of how much my late sister loved them, too. So, to all of the special characters in this book and to our Five Star author, let's give this book: FIVE GOLDEN BUTTERFLIES TO BRING JOY TO EVERYONE WHO READS THIS NOVEL.

CURRENT CREEK VALLEY

Author: RaeAnne Thayne
Series: Hope's Crossing #4
Page count: 315
ISBN: 978-1611733471
Formats: Large Print, Paperback, ebook
Find the author:
www.RaeanneThayne.com

REVIEW BY FRAN LEWIS

Hope's Crossing might be a quiet town filled with hard working people, but when Sam Delgado and Alexandra McKnight meet, the sparks fly, the chemistry is hot, and the electricity is more powerful than the lightning in an electrical storm.

As Alexandra is about to embark on a career as a sous-chef in a new restaurant being built in town, she faces many obstacles when designing the kitchen. The first is Sam Delgado, and ex-Army Ranger and the foreman of the construction company who she mistakes for a mugger, killer, and all-around bad guy when she finds him in the restaurant. The scene is hysterical, and you just won't believe what she does when he tries to explain who he is and why he's there. Imagine someone bashing you with a board. That gets more than his attention. When he explains the reason why he's there, the cat never gets her tongue but the flirtation bug does.

As Alexandra gets herself out of an uncomfortable situation, she realizes that there is definitely something between them. Only time or quick thinking can tell what the final outcome will be, but there is much more to learn.

Alexandra's sister Maura owns the bookstore, which many of her friends frequent for coffee and the book club that allows them to talk about their favorite authors and books. Another sister owns String Fever, which provides a great way to express one's artistic abilities.

It's a small town and everyone knows just about everyone else, and even the gossip mongers have their own take on Alexandra, some not so pleasant. When she manages to very bluntly ask Sam out, then goes with him to the Speckled Lizard to shoot pool, one young girl is anything but thrilled to see her. We also learn about Sam's secret, which he does not want to divulge to Alexandra, as well as his hopes for his future. There's also a hint about her past and the kindnesses she and others are performing for her elderly friend, Caroline, and several other people in her town who cannot prepare meals and take care of themselves.

As their first date is about to come to a close, they see a what they think is a stray dog. She asks her brother, the chief of police, to put out the word to find the owner of the chocolate Labrador she's named Leo.

In this town, no one can keep a secret and gossip is rampant. Her new restaurant seems to be creating a lot of hype even before it opens. Someone spies her with the hot guy she is out with, and now her mother wants to know what gives and so does the rest of the town, just as Alex learns her mother's news about getting married to a man that Alex is not sure is right for her mother but has learned to accept.

The town seems to be buzzing and romance is in the air, so why is Alexandra avoiding Sam? She can't avoid him forever. He has dinner at her restaurant and is in food heaven from her cooking. He also meets the man her mother is going to marry, Harry Lange. Lange, the major shareholder in the Silver Strike Resort Group, makes Sam tense for reasons he can't identify.

Things start to heat up even more when Sam decides to settle in Alexandra's town and brings along his son for some house hunting. When the realtor flirts with Sam, trying to get a reaction from Alexandra, she realizes Sam just might be fair game. Will she stand by and let the realtor snap him up?

Confessions of the heart and the past occur, and Alex and Sam start to open up to each other. Sam explains what caused the rift between him and his late wife's parents, which only makes him like Alexandra more even though she continues to push him away.

Caroline, her older friend, might change her perspective, explain life to her, and send her on the trail of real happiness. Taking a chance in life, listening to Caroline might take away some of the pain and the fear she has of finding a new relationship, but taking that step forward is something Alexandra needs to do on her own.

Can one ex-soldier with a great seven-year-old son convince this stubborn and hardheaded young woman they are right for each other? What about her mother's marriage to Harry?

This story combines loyalty, honesty, fear, and betrayals from the past, and memories that won't fade in a town with secrets but filled with love. When the realities set in will Alexandra turn away from Sam and send him to someone else? Will Sam be able to convince her to let him into her life? Will she heed her friend's final words: Go, Live, Love.

In the end, secrets are revealed, truths told, and one young woman's life hangs in the balance. Readers are treated to an ending that will surprise them and a town that just might make you want to move there. What is the final outcome? What will Alex decide to do? Will she run or will she finally realize that she's already where she belongs? Once again, author RaeAnne Thayne takes us on a journey into a town that has its faults, but just might be picture-perfect.

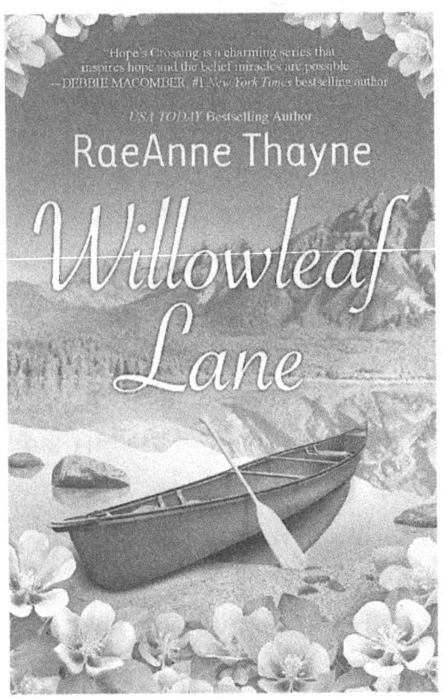

WILLOWLEAF LANE
Author: RaeAnne Thayne
Series: Hope's Crossing #5
Page count: 384
ISBN: 978-0373777693
Formats: Large Print, Paperback, ebook
Find the author: www.RaeanneThayne.com

REVIEW BY FRAN LEWIS

Forgiveness...wrongly accused or just a victim of circumstances, many people find themselves ostracized by past mistakes. Sometimes those mistakes are no fault of their own, while others will come back and haunt them. When Peyton Gregory enters Sugar Rush and makes small talk with Charlotte, little do either of them realize that the past is about to resurface in the present and old feelings are about to come to the forefront.

Spencer and Charlotte were never really friends but managed to form an alliance when they were kids. Charlotte, who was overweight and subject of teasing and rude comments from other kids, befriended Spencer, whose past was not much better than most kids who came from a poor family. Because he is good at sports, he finally soars above his circumstances has a lucrative career in baseball until everything falls apart.

Accused of selling steroids and drugs to his teammates, Spencer lost his sponsors, credibility, and the respect of those living in Hope's Crossing. So, when he saunters into Sugar Rush to find his daughter who has come in looking for a sweet treat, needless to say, Charlotte is anything but pleased.

The town is gossiping about his sudden arrival and the fact that Harry Lange made him director of the new recreation center. Some people question Harry's sanity and wonder why he would do such a thing. But those who know and love Harry understand that hiring the best man for the job is his motive, and he's willing to give him another chance. Harry never really cared what others think.

Charlotte and Spencer have a short, curt, and uneasy conversation as he begins to recall that he knew her in the past but cannot believe how amazing she looks in the present, and Charlotte won't admit that she is taken with Spencer.

Going for her morning run, Charlotte never expects to literally run into Spencer, sprain her ankle, and injure her hand. Like a knight in shining armor, Spencer literally carries her home, much to her chagrin. She learns more about why he is in town, and hears his daughter Peyton's take on things, and she begins to wonder if what the gossips are saying about him is true.

Eventually his past is revealed and he admits to working for Charlotte's father. Then something causes everyone in the town to wish he'd never returned. The reader is left wondering what is true. We learn about Spencer's late wife, Jade, and their dysfunctional relationship, and her suspicious death. Now everyone in Hope's Crossing thinks he's responsible for his wife's drowning.

Before you can accept forgiveness you have to learn to forgive yourself and deal with your own problems head on. As Charlotte and Spencer's paths seemed to cross more often, they begin to realize that old feelings might be ignited. A simple comment by Peyton sets off an amazing chain of events, proving to Spencer how the town comes together when they feel a cause is worthwhile. But, sometimes other things get in the way of success, and you are blindsided by an issue that you were not aware of or just didn't see.

Peyton and Spencer both have secrets. When attending a beading class with some young teens, something happens that makes Charlotte think that Peyton might be hiding something that needs to be addressed. Relating her thoughts to Spencer creates tension, but might open his eyes in more ways than one. Once again, Maura, Katherine, Harry, Dermot, and many others come together to hopefully create an event that will spearhead Spencer's project: Warrior's Hope.

The story has an ending that will surprise you and plot that will endear you to everyone in Hope's Crossing. Will Charlotte allow her heart to win out or will she run away? Will Peyton find her way back and realize that healing comes with work? Will Spencer's name ever be cleared? Will he stay?

The author also tackles some serious subjects like eating disorders, and brings to light what happens when one a teen faces so many problems in her young life that she fails to see what is happening to her. There are many warning signs the author relates in this novel, and there are many lessons to be learned by everyone.

Author RaeAnne Thayne takes us inside the hearts and minds, of this town and shows the kindnesses that abound in a town everyone would love to live in. Forgiveness, loyalty, trust, faith, family, and hope are the powerful themes in this outstanding Five Star Novel.

ABOUT THE RAEANNE THAYNE

I'm not one of those people who knew from birth she was destined to become a writer. I always loved to read and throughout my childhood I could usually be found with a book in my hands. To the disgust of my friends, I even enjoyed creative writing assignments that made them all groan. But I had other dreams besides writing. I wanted to be an actress or a teacher or a lawyer.

Life took a different turn for me, though, when my mother made me take a journalism elective in high school (thanks, Mom!). I knew the first day that this was where I belonged.

After I graduated from college in journalism, I took a job at the local daily newspaper and I reveled in the challenge and the diversity of it. One day I could be interviewing the latest country music star, the next day I was writing about local motorcycle gangs or interviewing an award-winning scientist.

Through it all — through the natural progression of my career from reporter to editor — I wrote stories in my head. Not just any stories, either, but romances, the kind of books I have devoured since junior high school, with tales about real people going through the trials and tribulations of life until they find deep and lasting love.

I had no idea how to put these people on paper, but knew I had to try — their stories were too compelling for me to ignore. I sold my first book in 1995 and now, more than 40 books later, I've come to love everything about writing, from the click of the computer keys under my fingers to the "that's it!" feeling I get when a story is flowing.

I write full-time now (well, as full-time as I can manage juggling my kids!) amid the raw beauty of the northern Utah Mountains.

Even though I might not have dreamed of being a writer when I was younger, now I simply can't imagine my life any other way.

LILLY STEPS OUT
Author: Rita Plush
Page count: 208
ISBN: 978-1935563891
Formats: Paperback, ebook, Audible Audio Edition
Find the author: www.RitaPlush.com

REVIEW BY FRAN LEWIS

What is the definition, according to Leon Gold, of a Wife? Maid, housekeeper, bed partner, organizer, cook, cleaner, and definitely someone that is there to take care of his needs. Well, maybe this fits someone living in prehistoric times but definitely not Lily Gold. Lily Gold might be over fifty, but she is not down and out yet. With a mind of her own she decides to change things up, but in her favor, not Leon's. When Leon retires, he thinks that things are going to remain the same. He can lounge around all day while Lily continues to service him in any way he sees fit. Inviting their son Larry over for dinner to celebrate his newfound freedom and retirement, Lily relates her plans for her own future. But, being a typical male, Leon thinks she is going through some kind of hormonal imbalance, not thinking clearly, and definitely does not take her seriously. But, when Lily decides to do something, watch out! Going through the want ads, walking the hot pavement, and looking for a job is not easy for someone her age. But, Lily is smart and enterprising, and when she just happens to walk by an antique shop, enters, and dazzles the owner with her knowledge, well… Lily is now a working girl, and Leon will just have to get over it!

Not really thinking that she will stick it out, he cannot believe how much she loves what she is doing and how good she is at her job. But Walter, her boss, seems kind of strange when people first meet him, and will sell only to people that he wants to, and often sales are lost… but not because of Lily. What happens next will definitely make you laugh and will endear you to Lily even more. Wait until you hear her innermost thoughts at a dinner party and meet their superficial and rich friends. Some think that Lily is having a mid-life thing, and Leon's sarcasm at the party gets him in trouble. But Lily gets even! Priceless! Many of the women talk about their vacations, their plans to renovate their homes, or how they are really good at spending their husband's money. But, Lily has other plans and when out one evening in midweek, wait until you find out what hot and heavy Lily decides to get Leon to do and where!

Lily is definitely committed to her new job and becomes so involved with creating a new window that she loses track of time, upsets Leon, and decides to stay out all night and not admit to where she stayed. On the way to finding a place to stay she meets Rusty, owner of an upscale boutique that most women would love to browse through and be able to afford the prices. But, Rusty makes it sound like she wishes she could trade places with Lily and have her life and a Leon of her own. Lily is definitely discontent with her life and cannot seem to find a happy medium. Her job is time consuming, fulfilling, and energizes her, and her marriage is taking a slow crash. Leon is about to do something that will definitely surprise not only the reader but Lily too. As the author flashes back to when they first met, her mother's reaction to him, his job, and his dedication, you begin to wonder if she is not doing the same thing Leon did before he retired. Can she come up with an even balance? What about Walter and the unique way he runs his shop? The author then enlightens readers as to why Lily questions Leon's whereabouts at times, recalling with a friend what happened between him and a woman named Fiona, and finally the end result with her son coming back home to live. Understanding her point of view, yet floundering on his own, Larry makes you wonder whether he is truly independent or just wants someone to direct his movements. Hoping for the approval of his parents, he never seems to remain in one job and falls back on them when things get tough. Lily seems to be let out of a cage or maybe squatting at the start line of a marathon race, and once the gun goes off she keeps running until she gets to the finish line. But, what happens when she gets there? Will she turn around and go back the way she came or will she keep on running? Can you run away from your life when things change? Marriages never remain the same and couples either grow together or grow apart. What will happen to Leon and Lily? That still remains to be seen.

Lily is determined to succeed in her job and Leon decides they need their own space. Trying to share her enthusiasm with him fails as she encourages her boss, Walter, to consider moving his store, finding merchandise he can part with, and then revitalizing his business as partners. Flashing back to their past, feelings come out and many resentments are heard as Lily and Leon try to mend what might be permanently damaged. Like a sculptor who takes a piece of clay and molds it to perfection and then decides to remold it again because nothing is ever truly perfect the first time, will Leon and Lily try to do the same with their lives, or will the clay piece get permanently tossed away?

Lily has her own idea of what she wants and forges ahead, much to the surprise of her friends, Leon, and her son. Wanting to start her own business requires some creative financial thinking. Knowing that her house is in her name and that she could use it as collateral is her ticket to her future. But, what Leon does throws more than just a nail in a damaged wall, and the end could be near for both of them.

Walter proves to be more than just a boss but a loyal friend, and we meet Miss Douglas, the owner of a house that would be perfect not only for Lily but for other businesses too. Just how this all pans out and whether she finally gets what she wants you have read to find out. Added in we hear Lily's own thoughts stated in italics, and we learn more about Leon, his wanderings, and his father Theodore.

This book is about change, taking a new turn in life, and being able to understand that not everything stays the same. As Walter and Miss Douglas face their own fears and have to decide whether to keep everything status quo or take a chance on Lily Gold and forge ahead, another member of the Gold family does the same. Hard feelings, sarcasm, selfishness, and pride are not only the traits of Larry Gold but Leon too. When the final signature has to be placed on the lease, will Lily be able to come up with the cash after what Leon did?

Filled with humor, sarcasm, and true to life events, all of which might bring some tears to the readers' eyes, *Lily Steps Out* is a vividly depicted novel written by author Rita Plush, who allows readers to hear the voices of each character loud and clear as the narrator sets the stage for the action to come. Each chapter can fill an episode of a made for television movie as readers will learn just how far Lily steps out and whether she decides to ever reverse and step back in!

Let's give this book: FIVE GOLDEN LILYS

INTERVIEW WITH RITA PLUSH

Please tell our readers something about yourself.

I am an author, teacher and interior designer. *Lily Steps Out,* Penumbra Publishing May 2012, is my first novel. My short stories appeared in many literary journals including *The Alaska Quarterly Review, The Iconoclast, The MacGuffin* and *Passager,* before they were published as a collection (*Alterations,* May 2013). I have lectured on interior design and the decorative arts at libraries throughout Long Island, at Hofstra University and CW Post-Hutton House. As the Coordinator of the Interior Design & Decorating Certificate at Queensborough Community College, I teach several courses in the program.

Please give our readers a brief summary of the book.

Lily Steps Out is a middle-age coming-of-age, the story of a suburban housewife who is sick of making beds and fixing breakfast and decides to step out of the comfortable domestic life she knows into the business world, much to the mocking disbelief of her loving husband, Leon, now retired, and their grown son, both perfectly content with The Way Things Are.

Not only does Lily love her work in an antique store, but when she decides to turn an old frame house into an antique center — she'll sublet the rooms to different vendors to cut down on her costs. But when she tells Leon her game plan, not only does he pooh-pooh the idea, but by the time she gets to their joint savings account to withdraw the lease money, Leon has cleaned it out. "This is trust?" she asks herself. "This is marriage? No! This is war!" With a little help from her friends Lily steps out of the tired old habit of always letting Leon have his way. And, while she's at it, she breaks the mold of Lily Gold. This time she turns the status quo into quid pro quo and gives Leon a run for the money. Lily's journey is the journey of every woman who wants love, respect and personal fulfillment.

The main character is Lily Gold: What adjectives would describe her and why?

Lily is feisty and yet introspective. Even when she decides to start her own business she worries about the effect it will have on her marriage. She is caring and dedicated to her family. Leon and Larry have always come first in her life. She's funny and her interior monologues bear this out.

Married for over 30 years to Leon, what causes her to want a change, get a job and feel emancipated?

Leon's retirement is a big "wake up and smell the coffee" moment for Lily. Is this all there is? Him parked in a husband's chair in Loehmans while she goes through the racks? Trailing after her in Waldbaums, "Do we need toilet paper?" "This cucumber or that one?" She is suffocating.

If Leon could speak to our readers, how would he define Lily's role in his life? How does his definition differ from hers?

I'd be lost without her, he'd say. She's everything to me. Friend, lover, confidant and helpmate. Lily would define herself the same way, but she wants to help herself now, break the old mold and create a new one.

Why did Leon seem to feel she was just going through some phase and would get over it?

Lily has spoken about getting a job before, even going back to school to get a college degree, but she's never followed through.

How did she finally get a job and where?

She goes through the want ads, then store to store till she lands a job with Walter Margolis.

How would you describe her boss Walter? What was odd about him and why?

Walter is a very troubled man. A terrible tragedy has tied him to his past and he's lived almost monk like till Lily arrives on the scene. He can be irritating and confrontational, yet he is immediately taken with Lily's spirit when she walks into his shop.

Describe the antique shop and how Lily took charge of changing its appearance.

More mausoleum than business, the contents of the shop are the furnishings of his childhood home, a real mess, a mishmash of periods and styles all piled and stacked together without rhyme or reason. Once Lily gets her capable hands on it, it's organized into neatly arranged aisles, every item clearly labeled and priced.

How did a store window set off a chain of events that would awaken Lily to turn her life in a different direction?

By hand picking objects from the conglomeration in his store and arranging them in an eye catching and artistic manner in his display window, Lily discovers a creative side of herself she hasn't known was there. She's made something from nothing. It is a true awakening for her.

Who is Rusty and how and why did they meet?

Rusty is the owner of a posh accessory store. She is closing up shop when Lily pulls to the curb and asks for instructions to the Downtown Inn.

Why did they form an instant bond?

They're both very open and genuine people, and they sense this about each other.

What was odd about where she spent her first night alone? How did this Inn play an integral part in the events to follow?

The Inn Lily where stays is part of the Downtown Renovation. It's still under construction, unfinished, in a way like Lily, who is also under construction, going through her own personal renovation, but by not letting Leon know where she is staying the night the event becomes the turning point in their relationship.

Who was Ms. Douglas, and what was her role in creating the changes Lily wanted in her life?

It's *Miss* Douglas. *Ms.* is too much of a contemporary appellation to be used with her name. She would bridle at that. Miss Douglas owns the old frame house at the Downtown Renovation that Lily wants to rent and turn into an antique center. It's Miss Douglas's willingness to accept the statuette of the gypsy dancer as collateral instead of cash to satisfy the terms of the lease that allows Lily to move forward with her plan.

Both Walter and Miss Douglas were steadfast about certain things: What? Why?

Both Walter and Miss Douglas have definite ideas about the way they want their business affairs run and when these tough cookies come up against each other, sparks do fly. Walter can only be pushed so far in negotiating Lily's lease, and he's willing to compromise in the rent increases just so much. Miss Douglas insists that the wallpaper must remain, and that she must approve other cosmetic changes in the house. Walter and Miss Douglas both have emotional ties to the houses in which they grew up.

When Lily asked Walter why he hired her, how does he respond and why did she ask him that question?

There comes a point in the story when Lily is very frustrated because Walter won't let her sell his merchandise, and it dawns on her that he probably never will. When she asks him why he hired her, he tells her that he liked her spirit, and that she brought new life into his shop.

What was her innovative idea and what reaction does she get from Leon? Why?

She realizes their house is in her name, and she decides to charge Leon rent for living there. Not only rent now, but back rent since he put the house in her name, years and years ago. Leon goes ballistic. He doesn't care whose name the house is in. It's *his* house.

How would this give her some freedom from her old life?

She'd then have the startup money for her own antique business.

Lily Gold was determined to forge ahead: What made her realize that her life with Leon might not continue or lead to a permanent Happily Ever After?

Every time Leon promises her money he either reneges on it, or he gives her less than they agreed on.

What did Leon do that was underhanded and might affect her business venture and their life together?

As soon as she told him she wanted to open an antique center and that she needed money to buy merchandise, he ran to the bank and withdrew all the money. How could she trust a man like that?

If Lily could speak to our readers, how would she answer these questions?

a. **When did you realize that Leon was hiding something, and how does he react when you reveal the truth?**

When I went down to the basement to look for the deed to the house and I found the old stock statements. We had much more money than I'd ever thought. He got defensive about it. He tried to tell me he was worried about not having enough for his retirement. Did he think I'd spend it all? I still get upset when I think about it.

b. **What was his reaction to your wanting to create your own business?**

At the beginning he thought it was a joke, then when he knew I was serious, he did everything he could to stop me.

c. **What roadblocks did he put in your way and why?**

He went right to the bank and cleaned it out when he knew I was serious. And when I put the house on the market he threw the broker out of the house. Just my luck, they were cleaning the pool at the gym and he came home early.

d. **How would he define your role in his life, and would he ever accept the new you?**

I had a very important role in his life, but bread-winner wasn't one of them. Leon was very happy with The Way Things Are — I think most men are like that—and it really threw him into a tailspin when I wanted to change the balance in our relationship. He's ready to kick back and take it easy, and his little woman is ready to set the world on fire.

e. **Are you sorry you did not do this sooner? Why or why not?**

I suppose a part of me is, and yet I wasn't ready for it sooner. I was content with my life until I wasn't, and then I did something about it. There's no point in regrets—it doesn't really get you anywhere.

Interior design is something that Lily is really good at: How does this mirror Rita?

Rita has been an interior designer for more than thirty-five years.

If you and Lily could come face to face and were given the same job to redecorate a store window or an entire house, would you do it the same way? Why or why not?

I've been in the field for much longer than Lily so naturally I bring more to the table, but Lilly is eager to learn, so I think we'd get along really well. I think we'd play off each other. She has such an enthusiasm about her new found vocation. I think she'd be a pleasure to work with. And she loves Art Deco (the gypsy dancer is from that period) my favorite decorative arts period.

How does Lily show she is a smart negotiator and businesswoman?

She's able to convince Walter to rent her his display window so she can start selling her own merchandise from there. She rents out Miss Douglas's house to different vendors so she doesn't have to absorb the rent on her own.

If Leon could answer these questions.

a. **In the end, Leon, what message would you give other men in your position?**

Fight the good fight, guys, but in the end, don't be surprised if you lose. Especially if you're married to a gal like Lily.

b. **What would you change about your past and yourself that might have resulted in a different outcome?**

I could have been more open with Lily about the money, but I was scared. Scared of change, scared of losing her to this new business. Who she might meet? Maybe someone she liked more than me. Maybe that doesn't make sense, us being married so long, having so much history. But feelings don't always make sense, do they?

c. **How does your past reflect on the present?**

I'm a macho guy from the old school. You know, aggressive, breadwinner, protector—though it doesn't look like my Lily needs too much protecting right now—and that's hard for me to change. But I could, if Lily would give me another chance. Hear that Lil?

What is next for Rita? What is your next novel and are you going to continue Lily's story?

At the moment, I'm trying to find an agent and/or publisher for my second novel, *Feminine Products,* which follows the relationship of Rusty and Walter. I'm also taking one of the stories in *Alterations,* my recently published short story collection, and developing it further. Maybe it will be another novel. The way I'll find out is to keep writing about the characters. As far as Lily goes, I have been thinking about her and her relationship with Leon. If they do get back together, I need drama and conflict and something at stake, after all, those are the elements that keep readers turning pages. Actually, writing about them just now has given me some ideas. What if ... I better not say.

Where can readers learn more about you, your work and your titles?

My website would be a good place to start www.ritaplush.com and my Facebook page

BOOK REVIEWS

MEANS TO AN END

Author: Elizabeth Romero
Page count: 356
ISBN: 978-1-62652-041-7
Formats: Paperback, ebook
Find the author: www.ElizabethRomeroBooks.com
Star rating: 

REVIEW BY FRAN LEWIS

Two women's lives are bound together who will never find their way to freedom as Marie Broudreaux pays a heavy price for one mistake that her family will never forgive. Imagine being trapped in a round cage of iron, and sitting within the confines of this cage with limited resources, little money, and no means of escape, as if you were a slave or in a circus. You are treated to frequent beatings and abuse at the hand of the master because you failed to meet his standards or just because he feels like venting his anger.

Married to Garrett after her father literally sold her into bondage for being pregnant with twins, Marie Broudreaux pays a heavy price for her one big mistake. Now her daughter, Ashby Devereaux lives her life in fear of Garrett, who revels in abusing her and her mother every way possible.

Cruelty seemed to make Ashby's stepfather feel like a man, and abusing Ashby and her brother, Danny, was his way of venting. A drunkard, thief, and pretty much worthless, he wielded his intensions on his stepdaughter without any regard for the consequences or her feelings.

Mrs. Bass, one of Ashby's teachers, realizes Ashby is going through something at home, but doesn't tell anyone. When Ashby is chosen Queen of the Carnival at school, she realized that she'll have to endure insults from the popular girls because she's poor. A young man named Bobby changes how she feels about herself, but that's short-lived. With nowhere to turn and a mother who is addicted to drugs and always out of it, and this poor young girl living in the backwards mountains of North Carolina has to fend for herself and pray for her own salvation.

When Garrett is arrested and does a stint in jail, Ashby sees this as a positive sign. But Johnny Mac, her stepfather's friend, wants to use her to repay a debt he claims Garrett owes him. By this point, Ashby has changed. Something within her caught fire and she will no longer allow anyone to use her for a punching bag or intimate fun. Before she can leave her unhappy home, she reveals something to her mother about Garrett and the incident turns ugly resulting in her being sent far away from her home never to return.

As the cage begins to open and Ashby might finally be free, something within her holds her back. Can she leave her mother to clean up the mess she created? Will the law come after her as she makes her way to New Orleans to find her grandparents? Will she connect with her long-lost brother?

The author explores the question: Can you hide from your past by changing who you are in the present?

Finding herself all alone on the streets of New Orleans, Ashby is befriended by someone who directs her to a rooming house and hopefully a job. But, oversleeping gets her fired, and another job comes to light as she moves to The Smoking House, where she can either become one of the working girls or a maid. Opting to become a maid and change her name to Monique, she is and befriended by Ms. Blanche, the proprietor, and draws the amorous attention of a local judge. Given the option of remaining with Ms. Blanche or moving in with the judge, she seeks advise from a friend about what to do to keep herself safe.

Getting to know the judge and wanting to please him kept Monique/Ashby content. But, in the back of her mind she knew that someone was after her and that the law might catch up with her, and the end result could change things for her forever. Never thinking that the judge might know about her past or that this could be a setup from the start, she moves into his home, is befriended by Corinne, his maid and cook, and the rest still remains to be seen. Abuse never leaves you, and the fear of being with any man still gives her the chills.

As Monique/Ashby gets to know Bradley, the undertone within their relationship allows readers to know that smooth sailing is not in the cards for them. He enlists help to learn more about her, but why? While she becomes more comfortable in her surroundings and closer to Bradley, she still has the fear of being found out.

As the authorities head in Monique's direction, she overhears a conversation and decides to run away once more. With the help of her friend, Bebet, she hopes to remain hidden and safe. Bradley forces both of their hands, though. What will be the final outcome?

What will be the fate of this young girl? Will the truth about Garrett's death ever come out? What were Marie's final words? What happens when a parent can't protect her children? The answers will bring tears to your eyes. The conclusion is filled with unexpected twists and surprises. The epilogue gives us a glimpse into her future and we hope the author will bring Monique Boudreaux back. This is one novel that brings to light what happens when secrets are kept, fear is instilled, abuses of many types are inflicted on so many, the tragic results. Sometimes the things we do are the only way to survive, or a *Means to An End*!

HOME WRECKER

Author: Brenda Perlin
Page count: 274
ISBN: 978-1462653898
Formats: Paperback, ebook
Find the author: www.HomeWreckerTheBook.com
Star rating: 

REVIEW BY FRAN LEWIS

Stand in front of a mirror and look closely at the image that is reflected back at you. The face that you are looking at has weathered many storms and might even have some wrinkles or worry lines, but the person staring back is still YOU! Acceptance of who we are is not always so cut and dried for some people. Others might chastise, criticize, and even ridicule us for the way we look, our attitudes, or even our manner of speech or expression. Standing tall, steadfast, and looking past what others think is difficult for a young child that is expected to live up to her parent's expectations and standards. When you meet Brooklyn Rosen as she unravels the many layers of her personality, life, and goals within this novel titled *Home Wrecker*, you will find that the image that is projected or reflected in the mirror has many different sides, and can be viewed from many different angles, but in the end it is still Brooklyn.

Relationships did not come easy for Brooklyn, and dealing with many of her family members brought out her many different sides. Her mother was her champion, her constant, and seemed to center her and bring out her fun and joyous side. Her father was tough, hardnosed, and often made her feel like she was really not living up to his standards. Her sisters were different, hoping to be close, but situations put strains on their relationships and they withered away. Starting with her first job and moving on from there, we learn much about Brooklyn, her goals, thoughts, and hopes for her future. When someone finally put a camera in her hands the world changed, her energy level rose, and things started to fall into place. But, she was not there yet. Many boyfriends, some good some bad, distancing herself from her father after losing her mother to cancer, and then finding out that many experiences in life would cause her to change are just some things that the author relates to the reader about Brooklyn. Waitressing, acting, and the combination of both careers seemed to fuel her for a while. Leaving both and then deciding to teach at a gym seemed to bring her some friendships and teach her a lot about people; and then something snapped and things went downhill.

Everyone wants what he or she cannot have at times, but we need to wait until we can afford to get them. Finding herself in a jail cell after stealing a dress, then confronted by the guard who took her in, Brooklyn hopefully learned some hard lessons. Meeting and dating different men would give her several different perspectives, including that of many others, but in reality she needed to decide for herself and listen to her inner most thoughts.

Her short attention span would hinder her from finding her real passion. Smart and astute in her own way, even though she did not realize it, Brooklyn's outlook and assessment of herself was probably harsher than that of friends or family. Never pushed to excel or do anything, Brooklyn needed to develop her self-discipline. Turning thirty brought its own hang-ups and issues, and a new decade that would hopefully bring out her strengths and stop playing on what she thought were her weaknesses. Flashing back to her thoughts about her mother she realized and reflected on the important things she was taught. Being who she was, not worrying about what others thought of her, and not trying to be like everyone else were great points to remember. Her relationship with Gerard and meeting his family brought mixed emotions, perceptions, and feelings; was he the right man for her? Why did she experience so many physical issues when preparing for her wedding to Gerard, which should have been happy? The difficulty with the dress, the decisions made, the wedding, the stress, and the final vows are all part of problem. Now, let's learn the rest.

Her father was with a woman named Lina, whose family was great at first, but then things changed when he became sick. Lina wanted money to live in the style to which she was accustomed…or you might say a huge slice of the pie. Greedy, not understanding yet wanting things, her father said to give her anything she wanted. Having money from her first husband and really not lacking for anything, then learning Brooklyn's father had cancer; Lina wanted his money for her kids. Brooklyn and Gerard took care of him, a man that just wanted his family to care about him. Both families, his (except Brooklyn and Gerard) and Lina's, came just for money, while all the while he was hoping someone would ask how he felt. His final days were spent with Brooklyn and Gerard.

Diagnosed with a disease like transverse myelitis, which is incurable, and then having to deal with doctors that often dismissed her concerns and the cause of her pain, Brooklyn did more than just weather her troubles. Gerard became distant, not really very supportive at times, and the end result was hospitalizations, therapy, medications, nurses that were not always compassionate, and fear of the unknown and what would happen next.

Anger, stress and lack of understanding can play havoc on a marriage and your life. Gerard's anger increased and his understanding diminished. So, how would Brooklyn deal with his mood changes, and what was next? But, she was a fighter and would not give up. Transverse myelitis is what she had do deal with, and using the Internet would help her to be equipped with more information and knowledge.

Life changed for her when she lost a friend to cancer and met a man name Bo at the gym. Although she remained married for a while longer, her relationship with Gerard seemed stilted, cold, and often disconnected. Revenge played a heavy part when someone felt they were wronged. The interactions between Brooklyn, Bo's wife, and Gerard are related in her own voice as you learn what happened when she decided to get divorced, and what Gerard did next. Threats, confrontations, anger, and much more would follow as things began to more than heat up for Brooklyn, who just wanted to be happy. Would Gerard let go? Would Bo's wife Ruth finally get the message and back off?

The ending will definitely make you think about the court system, about how truths get twisted, and about whether one woman named Brooklyn will come out alone, with another man she loves, or just bear the pain of the title *Home Wrecker*. After reading this book, hearing her words, finding out what happens, and the final verdict in the court case, make your own decision. Is she a home wrecker, or were both homes wrecked before Brooklyn and Bo met? This is one novel that will definitely give readers much pause for thought as you learn about betrayals, loyalties, guilt, friendships, and one woman's struggle just to find happiness.

REDEMPTION

Author: Troy Lambert
Page count: 266
ISBN: 978-1462653898
Formats: Paperback, ebook
Find the author:
TroyLambertWrites.com
Star rating: ★★★★★

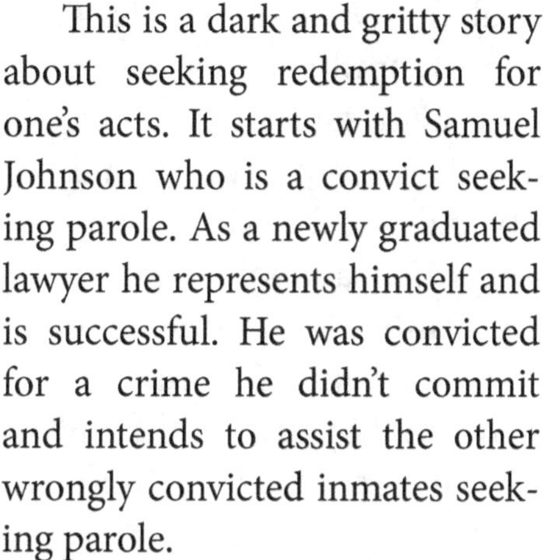

This is a dark and gritty story about seeking redemption for one's acts. It starts with Samuel Johnson who is a convict seeking parole. As a newly graduated lawyer he represents himself and is successful. He was convicted for a crime he didn't commit and intends to assist the other wrongly convicted inmates seeking parole.

Fast forward to the case of Arthur, Randy and Sally. Arthur has been lusting after Sally since high school. However Sally is now married to Randy and they have two children. Arthur is plotting something to get Sally back.

Long story short, bad things happen and Samuel Elijah Johnson, attorney at law is called in to represent Sally who has been framed.

I found the story to be well written with deep religious undertones. I found Sam to be an interesting character. He is trying hard to be professional as a lawyer but his old ways shine through occasionally and that gives the dark plot a bit of comic relief. I would recommend this book to suspense lovers and happily give it 5 stars.

REVIEW BY KAREN VAUGHN

DEAD MAN'S HAND

Author: Luke Murphy
Page count: 236
ISBN: 978-1-926997-88-9
Formats: Paperback, ebook
Find the author:
www.AuthorLukeMurphy.com
Star rating: 

Calvin Watters was NFL Superstar until a wrong move on the field caused an injury and also brought shame. At twenty-six he is now an enforcer for a bookie and is being framed for murder and marked for death. Fighting for his life and his girlfriend he is also trying to prove his innocence in three murders.

What's a man to do? Fight back and help the police solve the crimes.

Dead man's hand is a page-turner and a riveting account of one man's attempt to protect all he holds dear.

Detective Dale Dayton also has a lot at stake; chiefly his marriage and his career as one of LVPDs finest to solve a high profile murder of a casino owner and catch a killer.

The story is not just another casino boss war but a heart-felt story of how two very different men are trying to turn their lives around and discover what's really important.

The reader will hopefully root for the protagonists by the end of the story

I give this five golden footballs and police badges for great story telling.

REVIEW BY DELLANI OAKES

WHERE HAVE ALL THE POP STARS GONE VOLUME 1

Author: Jeff Marsh and Marti Smiley Childs
Page count: 322
ISBN: 978-1937317003
Formats: Paperback
Find the author on GoodReads
Star rating: 

REVIEW BY FRAN LEWIS

Listening to some of the great videos on YouTube before reviewing this book, I wanted to hear the music of The Buckinghams, Bobby Goldsboro, The Moody Blues, Sam and Dave, Ray Stevens, The Grass Roots, and Donnie Brooks. Jeff March and Marti Smiley Childs have definitely hit the top 100 charts with this collection of biographies of the each artist or group's rise to fame and where they are now. All too often we wonder what happened to some of the artists, movie stars, or TV personalities that we watched late at night or on Saturdays at the afternoon matinees. The authors provide a brief bio of each artist, and after the bio is a special tribute to each band member called the "Epilogue," which highlights their successes and careers.

Beginning with The Buckinghams, the author's highlight how they picked the right songs, their early days, and where it all began. For over two decades or more this outstanding group featuring Carl Giammarese, Nick Fortuna, Marty Grebb, and John Poulos, the original group members, graced stages and concert halls with their music, humor, wild performances, and well known sound. Fans went wild when they performed, and all too often it was difficult to hear the music and their voices as the crowds' cheers rang out. With the Beatles on the rise and taking England and America by storm, the Buckinghams had to create songs that would put them on the charts. "Kind of A Drag," gave them national exposure and put them as No. 1 on the charts, but not everything went smoothly and things did change after a while.

Although their manager Guercio propelled them to stardom, he also took actions that would alert them to the reverse, and they realized that their manager no longer had their best interest at heart. Perception is often quite powerful, and when they realized that the money was flowing in but not into their wallets, changes had to be made and they were. The "Portraits" album was their last chance to rise to the top. With top forty Billboard hits and audiences that filled chairs for more than two decades during the '60s and '70s, you can hear the rising cheers, listen to their sound, and realize that they were just a group of kids that loved music and formed something special. Listening to "Don't You Care" I just wanted to get up and dance, and "Mercy, Mercy, Mercy" — my personal favorite — really gets you moving. The authors completed the short bio with their comeback, their musical festival tours, and where they are now. Like a good mystery, if you want to learn more about them, their U.S. hit singles, and where they are now, you have to read the first section of

Where Have All the Pop Stars Gone? Volume 2 to find out.

Bobby Goldsboro was unique and different in his own right. He did not count on others to write his songs and compose his material. His career rocked and the talented performer of the '60s began as a guitar player with everyone's favorite singer, Roy Orbison. Only allowed to take one musician with him on tour, Bobby was chosen to go along with this icon. Imagine touring with him and being on the same stage as the Beatles. Bobby's first recording was made in Alabama and the song was called "Molly," which I listened to on YouTube, followed by another song that I wanted to hear titled "Honey." This song is beautiful, and seeing him perform it on YouTube really is really something. The words are just perfect. He had fifteen top forty hits, and imagine being booked to open for the Rolling Stones! "Honey" became his best selling hit, and he also formed the House of Gold Music, which published "Wind Beneath My Wings." As a songwriter he earned twenty-seven BMI awards and worked with Bette Midler, Paul Anka, and even Dolly Parton. Scoring major hits and moving to television, he syndicated the Bobby Goldsboro Show, which ran for three seasons, and became one of the highest rated variety shows.

Bobby's major goal was to write songs, and as great as creating records was, writing songs was what kept him alive and vital. He devoted more time to writing and producing children's entertainment, audio books and much more in the '80s. Where is he now? Read about his life, past, present and hopes for the future. "Can You Feel It" … a great song that I just listened to, but my favorite is "And I Love You So" from 1971. When they play this at weddings, I will remember that I heard it on YouTube today. The words are amazing and so meaningful.

Next, the authors introduce a group that I know little about, but I did listen to their music while writing this review … The Moody Blues. This group started as an R&B group. They began in Birmingham, England and were founded by Mike Pinder and Ray Thomas. Ray played harmonica and did vocals, and Mike also did vocals and the keyboards. Pinder did not remain with the band even though they were successful. The Moody Blues were unique in their sound, and Mike and Ray united with another band, the authors tell us, called the Krew Kats.

Going overseas to Germany, where rock bands ruled, and returning in 1963 to England, the musical scene had greatly changed and jobs and opportunities were limited. With new management, new promoters, and new members Denny Laine, Graame Edge, and Tony Secunda, their tours were booked and the band would play at the Marquee Club. As a result Decca Records picked them up. Their first record or single was "Steal Your Heart Away" in 1964. I did listen to it, and I think my favorite song that they recorded was "Twilight Time," followed by "The Voice" … the video is really amazing and quite graphic. While some of the members released solo albums, their joint album "Days of Future Passed" became more than just their trademark release … it made history for them, creating songs that infused both rock and classical sounds that would be new to listeners and to the record company too. But, before you read the book you really need to listen to the music to understand the time periods and the music they created. The rest and where they are now, you need to find out for yourself.

The lasts four artists are Donnie Brooks, Steve and Dave, Ray Stevens, and The Grass Roots. Donnie Brooks had two major hits, one being "Mission Bell," which was a huge success for him on Era Records and made it to number seven on the charts. Born in 1936, he passed away in 2007. Adopted when he was a teen by his stepfather, he took his name John Faircloth. "Bertha Lou" was recorded in 1959, and he made his first recording using the name Donny Brooks that same year. He achieved fame in 1971, and his career spanned over four decades. He was a great American pop singer.

Sam Moore and Dave Prater Jr. are next and are noted for being among the world's "most popular recording and performing artists, and with their frenzied stage appearances established themselves as the most electrifying duo in the history of rhythm and blues." With a sound that was unique to them and with hints of Sam Cooke, The Impressions, and Ben E. King, they soared.

Next, the authors included Ray Stevens, whose "Everything Is Beautiful" is still one of my favorite songs. Ray Stevens recorded romantic ballads. He was a recording session producer, music publisher, a session musician, disc jockey, and even the owner of a musical theater. He not only recorded ballads, but the author's share with readers that he also recorded pop music. Ray signed with Monument Records in 1968 and hit the Top 30 with "Mr. Businessman," and even turned down the chance to record with Burt Bacharach. Signing with Andy Williams's label, Barnaby, after appearing on his show, he hit the charts with "Everything is Beautiful," which was a huge hit and a Grammy Award Winner. "Mississippi Squirrel Revival," is really great, about sneaking a squirrel into church and the chaos that ensues. "Ahab the Arab" is hilarious, and so is the video.

Next, last but not least, The Grass Roots. They had tons of major hits like "Midnight Confessions," "Temptation Eyes," and "Where Were You When I Needed You?" They hit the top 40 charts and had seven gold singles and even one platinum one. The history behind this group and the biography is not that easy to relate because three groups created The Grass Roots. The Bedouins were one of the bands that were recruited, and the authors relate their story and how they became part of The Grass Roots within the first part of their section. After a series of comings and goings by group members, the new faces and new sounds kept them on the charts for over 307 weeks. The music is amazing, the history brings these groups to where they belong—the present—and kept me singing and dancing all afternoon while reading this outstanding FIVE PLATINUM RECORD BOOK. *Where Have All The Pop Stars Gone?* They are right here within this outstanding book with their bios, where they are now, and what some still hope for their futures. So, listen real hard and you just might hear your favorite song. The pictures added are timeless and priceless

REVIEW BY SUSAN ROSS

SONGS FOR PAPA CROW

Author: Marit Menzin
Page count: 32
ISBN: 978-0764341311
Formats: Hardcover
Find the author on Facebook
Star rating: ★★★★★

Summary: Little Crow loves to sing, and Papa Crow loves his song. But when Little Crow shares his crow songs with the other birds at the big old tree, they laugh and scatter. Maybe Mockingbird can teach him to sing songs with the finches, flycatchers, and cardinals and help him make some friends. But Little Crow should be careful what he wishes for...

Using Mockingbird's tip, Little Crow quickly becomes the most popular bird on the block. But, in a moment of danger, he learns that singing someone else's song can have terrible consequences and that his own voice and his father's love is of the greatest value.

Paired with colorful collage illustrations, this inspirational story is complemented by fun facts about North American birds and their sounds. Grades Pre-K to 2.

Review: This book centers around Little Crow who loves to sing and wanted to sing like other birds. Trying as hard with all of his ability and might, Little Crow did not succeed. Sometimes we might learn that we cannot do things the way others can and we have to accept who we are and ourselves. Little Crow learns many lessons in this outstanding book. When in danger wait and see which voice helps him and just might bring him to safety. Read Song for Papa Crow and find out.

REVIEWS BY SUSAN ROSS

KATIE WOO RULES THE SCHOOL

Author: Fran Manushkin
Page count: 96
ISBN: 978-1404879089
Formats: Paperback, ebook
Find the author on Facebook
Star rating: 

Short story chapter book that includes the stories Katie and the Class Pet, No More Teasing, The Big Lie and Star of the Show.

Summary: For Katie Woo, school is one big adventure. Join the stylish schoolgirl as she learns how to be a great classmate and friend. From the school play to the class pet, Katie knows how to rule the school!

Thought Questions posed by this book include:

What would you do if someone bothered you in school? How would you handle it and whom would you go to for help?

After reading this story think about what Kati did and decide whether you would do the same thing. What would you have done differently and what would you have done the same way?

What lessons can we learn from reading this book?

Write a letter to Kati and tell her what you think of how she handled the situation.

Elegy, Amanda Hocking

Divergent: Veronica Roth

The Book of Mysteries, Fran Orenstein

Looking for Alaska, John Green

To Kill A Mockingbird, Harper Lee

The Fault in Our Stars, John Green

The Book Thief, Marcus Zusak

Books, Books & More

Books, Books and More is the perfect place to search for that next cookbook, mystery, kids book and even history. You'll also find unique items that you probably won't find elsewhere. And everything is priced just right! So check through the listings and see what you might be missing.

All books and items are sold barely more what was paid for them. My main goal is to find a nice home for them and keep them in circulation. Many of the books are old and can be found in no other format, which means once they are gone they are gone forever.

Most items listed on this site are found at Estate Sales and due to that I have no way of knowing if the house had a smoker. I do everything I can to make sure there is no smoke smell and even musk smells attached to the vintage books and items.

Weight Watchers
Annual Recipes for
$2.50

Weight Watchers
Annual Recipes for
$2.50

Weight Watchers
Annual Recipes for
$2.50

Weight Wachers
Annual Recies for
$2.50

Central Africa
Republic Olympic
$3.00

Fujeira Zodia Stamps
(BMM-68)
$3.00

Sharjah Olympic
Winner Stamps (BBM-
$3.00

Cooking Light
Cookbook 1994
$3.00

Weight Watches
Quick Cooking for
$2.50

SPONSORED REVIEW

MEANS TO AN END

Author: Elizabeth Romero

Page count: 356

ISBN: 978-1-62652-041-7

Formats: Paperback, ebook

Find the author: www.ElizabethRomeroBooks.com

Star rating: ★★★★★

REVIEWS BY MARTHA A. CHEVES

Just as she was wrapping it around her, her stepfather appeared there in the doorway. She almost screamed because he startled her so. He had seen her naked before but not this way, only when he would sneak into her room in the dark. She slapped her hand to her mouth to keep from crying out as he slowly leaned back on the door that separated her form the hall.

"What...what are you doing in here? Momma will hear you," she said.

"That ole cow won't hear a thing. She done took a couple of her little pills and she is snoring up a storm. It is just you and me."

She suddenly realized that he was cold sober. She tried to reach for the doorknob, but he caught her arm. He was scary when he was drunk but not as quick.

Somehow this was different, and it was worse knowing he was in complete control now.

He pulled her near him and said, "You know we could be good friends if you weren't so uppity. I've been feeding the three of you since me and your momma came to Carolina. I reason you owe me a good time once in a while."

Ashby, her twin brother Danny and her mother Marie Boudreaux were sent to their own living hell when Ashby's grandfather sent her mother off to marry, not the twin's father, but Garrett Devereaux when he found she was pregnant with the twins. He made them leave New Orleans and sent them to a run-down home with forty acres of land that he had won in a horse race many years before. And he did this just to save face in the community.

Garrett, who required Ashby and Danny to call him Poppa, were in for the abuse that only a monster like Garrett could inflict. His hobby seemed to be getting drunk and then giving the kids and their mother a good beating. Danny finally had enough and ran away, Ashby assumed to New Orleans so she was left to protect herself. Her mother, who should have taken steps to keep her children safe spent most of her time popping pills and sleeping.

So now at the age of 17 Garrett has added another abuse to his list ... Sexual.

Following Ashby as she deals with not just Garrett but also the 'popular girls' at school who added their own abuse through calling her names and passing rumors, gave me a feeling of heartbreak and pain that a child like Ashby must go through just to survive. From what happens to Garrett to Ashby's chance of escape I had a hard time not reading just one more page and then just one more page in hopes that she would find some relief in her life. The events that take place through her survival makes this one of the most unforgettable books I've read in some time and I'm happy to say that there are at least 2 more books that will allow me to spend even more time with Ashby and her life.

Martha A. Cheves, Author of *Stir, Laugh, Repeat; Think With Your Taste Buds; A Book and A Dish*

Refrigerator Pickles

4-5 thinly sliced cucumbers
1 large thinly sliced red onion
1 large thinly sliced bell pepper
(color of your choice)
3 cups white vinegar
1-1/2 cups sugar
2 Tbsp. pickling spices
1 Tbsp. salt
2 canning jars (1 qt. each with lids)

In a large bowl combine vinegar, sugar, salt and spices. Stir making sure sugar dissolves completely. Evenly divide veggies into jars, packing tightly without breaking. Fill jars with vinegar mixture. Top with lid and refrigerate 24 hours. Can be kept in refrigerator up to 2 months.

Comments: This recipe originally called for less vinegar but I found I needed the extra cup to fill my jars. It also called for 1 tsp. celery flakes and 1 tsp. red pepper flakes. I decided to use the pickling spices instead. These "pickles" are so good. The red onion gives off just a touch of flavor heat. The pickling spices add the perfect flavors and the jars are really pretty. I did notice that the onions have a tendency of ending up on the bottom but they can be fished out when serving.

Also, I'm going to try using cheesecloth for the pickling spices instead of allowing them to be loose. That should give me the flavors without the actual spices being attached to my pickles. When I worked up my bell pepper I sliced it in half to remove the seeds and core, then sliced that in half to give me smaller, thinner pieces. This is one recipe that everyone who loves the Bread & Butter style pickles has raved about. I've also discovered that I can add more veggies to the liquid as the jar empties. Let them sit for 24 hrs. and you're ready to go again.

SUBMITTED BY MARTHA CHEVES

Crockpot Meatballs

1 pkg. store brand meatballs, Swedish, Angus or Italian — approx 78
1 bottle Compliments 3 Peppercorn and Brandy BBQ Sauce
1 bottle Diana sauce — original or spicy, depending on gastronomical sensitivity
1 10 oz. can of pineapple chunks, with Juice or buy the rings and do the work.
1 tbsp. more or less of curry powder — again ask yourself how brave you are

Brown meatballs in 400°F oven for 15 minutes, turning once. Place meatballs in crockpot and add the other ingredients. Cook for 3-5 hours. Serve with Rice or noodles. This recipe can be doubled or tripled.

Substitutes or Variations: Bottle of salsa, orange ginger dipping sauce. If you can't find the Compliments sauce — use Heinz Chili sauce.

SUBMITTED BY KAREN VAUGHN

Middle Man, David Rich
Means to an End, Elizabeth Romero
Lily Steps Out, Rita Plush
Clean Margins and Other Stories, Linda Rocker
Original Death, Eliot Pattison
Devil in the Hole, Charles Salzberg
Declan's Cross, Carla Neggers
The Warrior's Silence, Ord Elliot

REVIEWS & INTERVIEWS

MARK RUBENSTEIN INTERVIEWS M.J. ROSE

M.J. Rose is the international best-selling author of 13 novels and three non-fiction books. Her most recent novel, *Seduction*, has received rave reviews from *USA Today*, *Publisher's Weekly* and many others.

Ms. Rose launched her publishing career in 1998 when she self-published her first novel, *Lip Service*. Traditional publishers rejected it, uncertain about a novel that did not fit a distinct genre. So, she set up a website where readers could download the book, and began promoting it online. The novel was chosen as a selection by the Literary Guild/Doubleday Book Club and became the first e-book to be published by a mainstream publisher.

The rest is history.

Ms. Rose's recent novels focus on reincarnation and other supernatural phenomena. *The Recreationist*, the basis for the Fox television series *Past Life*, was followed by *The Memorist*, *The Hypnotist*, *The Book of Lost Fragrances* and now, *Seduction*.

How did you make the transition from advertising to writing novels?

When I was in advertising, I did a great deal of work on television commercials. A co-worker and I wrote a screenplay which led to a few more screenplays and some were optioned by production companies. I was advised to move to California, but didn't want to make the move. I decided to use another form of storytelling, so I wrote a novel.

Your last few novels, particularly *The Book of Lost Fragrances* and *Seduction* have dealt with reincarnation; the importance of the past; the collective unconscious and the power of memory. Can you share some of your thoughts concerning the importance of the past and memory?

I've always been fascinated by how the past impacts the present. For the first half of my career as a novelist, I wrote psychological suspense mysteries. I wanted to be a therapist but was told that while I was a fine diagnostician, I would be a terrible therapist because I wanted to solve everyone's problems.

So I wrote four novels about a New York City sex therapist. I then decided to write something historical because I was so interested in the past. I had an idea of writing novels that brought together the past and the present. I've always been fascinated by the concept of reincarnation.

I learned that many brilliant people were interested in reincarnation, including Carl Jung. I'm a big Jungian. So I began writing novels involving theories integrating past and present, even if the past element in the novel took place 500 or 1,000 years ago. They say every writer really just writes about one thing over and over. I guess my one thing is how the past impacts the present.

Is that how you feel about your own life and the lives of people you know?

I think so. I think that people can change. I've known people who have changed in therapy. I recall reading that those who do well in therapy tend to be people who would do well without therapy, too. They're bright, well-read, and educated. They also tend to be optimistic. However, on a certain level, you must live with your past. But your response to it can change.

Of course, when I'm writing, I'm simply trying to tell a story. I use the past as a trope. It's a fascinating way to explore someone's character and identity, trying to imagine who they might have been in the past, and how that might have affected them.

You mention exploring someone by imagining who they might have been in the past. Is there anyone you would love to have been?

I've never thought about that. I went to a past life therapist in my 20s because I was writing a screenplay about reincarnation. There was only one time when I was hypnotized deeply enough that I saw myself walking on a rocky path. I looked down and saw my shoes. They were the kind Pilgrims wore. That was the extent of my past life memory. Of course, that could be something I made up. We're capable of spinning amazing tales; after all, we're writers. So I don't know if I ever actually had a past life memory.

When I read *Seduction*, I felt you captured the voice of Victor Hugo exquisitely. You must have done an enormous amount of research for the novel.

I'd read about Victor Hugo believing in reincarnation and about his getting involved in séances to reach his dead daughter. I'd always known that one of the books in this series would involve Victor Hugo as the element of the past. I did a great deal of research about him and his having spent three years on the Isle of Jersey. He was writing *Les Miserables* at the time.

When I sat down to write the book, I just couldn't write. I suddenly realized I had taken on the most insane task in my life. Victor Hugo was one of the greatest novelists of all time. And I was going to write a novel in which one third of it would be him telling us about his séances in his own voice. I was worried it would be seen as an amazing kind of hubris to think I could write like Victor Hugo. After a few months of not being able to write, I called my agent and said I couldn't do it. I wanted to change the book and buy back the contract from the publisher. My agent came up with the idea of reading Hugo's letters because they were probably written in a more ordinary voice than his novels. I wouldn't be trying to write in the voice of a great French novelist if I read these more prosaic letters.

I read ten or fifteen letters of his. But I still couldn't write a word of the novel. Then, the strangest thing happened. I accidentally knocked over an antique jar of pens on my desk; one of the pens fell onto my laptop. I looked at it and had a flash.

I uncapped the pen and pulled out an unlined journal I'd bought in France. I dipped the pen in some ink, turned off the light, and began writing in natural daylight. I wrote in the voice of Victor Hugo, the way he wrote: with pen, ink and paper. The voice was there. I wrote 120,000 words, by hand, in journals. It was the first time I wrote a novel by hand.

In a Jungian sort of way, I felt I'd tapped into the collective unconscious and Victor Hugo's spirit. I must say, that when I typed the handwritten manuscript into the computer, I didn't remember writing any of the Victor Hugo part.

Reading *Seduction*, I was struck by the prominent role of olfaction — scents, fragrances and memories. Can you tell us a bit about that?

The olfactory center is next to the memory center of the brain. When you smell something, you can remember the moment in a far more clear and vivid way than when you see or hear it. Perfume was always in my life: my mother and grandmother were very loving. They also brought perfume back from Europe. I remember as a girl trying to make perfume from eucalyptus leaves. It really came together for me when I was in advertising and got involved with a campaign for a new fragrance. I became involved with the entire process of making a perfume, and no pun intended, it got under my skin.

When I began researching reincarnation, I learned, among other things, that the word *perfume* actually means *through smoke*. The ancient Egyptians believed the soul left the body and travelled on the smoke of incense to the afterlife. So perfume and spirituality were intrinsically connected. The more I read, the more involved I became.

When I write, I'm very conscious of the five senses. I now use them unconsciously; but I focused very consciously on them early in my career. I use them to create and experience characters. Various writers have different ways of exploring and creating characters. My first instinct is to describe what is seen, heard, tasted, felt and smelled.

Conventional wisdom says a writer should stay with a specific genre for commercial and other reasons. Your novels have been characterized as thrillers, paranormal novels, as Gothic, suspense and as historical thrillers. How have you managed to blend genres so successfully?

I just write the novels I want to read. It's hurt my career from a commercial point of view but not from a critical perspective.

If you want to be a successful commercial novelist, I wouldn't recommend doing what I did. But I decided early on, that the day I felt the pressure to mold what I was writing to make my books commercially viable, I would go back into advertising. I didn't want to write for the market, because that's what you do in advertising, where you get paid really well. I'd written three books about a New York City sex therapist. I felt that if I continued writing about that, it would get very stale for me. Everyone said I was making a terrible mistake; people loved the books and I was told I had a chance to make a franchise out of this character.

I felt I couldn't do it any longer. I've been very lucky: I wrote what I wanted to and have had publishers who have published my work. But the downside is I don't have a genre-specific following. The readers who loved the sex-therapy books didn't follow me into the metaphysical suspense novels, while those who enjoy what I now write aren't interested in me earlier work.

You mentioned you like writing the novel you want to read. Whom do you enjoy reading?

There's C.W. Gortner. I love Kate Mosse's books. Another is Kate Forsythe, an Australian writer. I love Lee Child's Jack Reacher books; Barry Eisler's John Rain books; Daniel Silva's Gabriel Allon novels. I enjoy reading Carol O'Connell; Allison Richmond; Daphne Du Maurier; F. Scott Fitzgerald and many others.

If you could have dinner with any writers or historical figures from any time in history, who would they be?

I would love to have Ayn Rand there because she's so controversial. I would want her to talk about the things she *doesn't* believe, and expose the Tea party for what it is. I would want Beethoven, F. Scott Fitzgerald, Jung, maybe Greta Garbo so I could learn some of her secrets. I think that would make for a great dinner party.

What would you be talking about?

I think we'd discuss how truly horrible our culture has become. There's so little innovation now, and we might talk about why so many people whine a great deal.

What advice, if any, would you give young writers today?

Writing is an *art* and publishing is a *business*. And it's a very broken business right now. I would tell every young writer a few things:

First and most important: write because you *love* writing, and for no other reason.

The press has made lots of noise about self-published writers, some of whom were created by companies wanting to encourage people to self-publish so they could become part of their business model. Now, Amazon is great — I love Amazon and owe them a great deal for helping my career. Amazon has helped level the playing field, and the company did direct marketing for some self-published authors to show how their books could become successful. The press picked up on this — making it look like it was easy to become a very successful self-published author. The truth is, it's incredibly difficult if you're starting out. I would advise young writers not to read the press.

You should only write if you can accept that you might reach only a few readers, one at a time; and that might be all you ever accomplish. You have to love the process of writing. The process is incredible. Writing is such an amazing and magical experience. If you can't *love* that, the rest of it is just too hard.

What's coming next from M.J. Rose?

I'm finishing a novel called *The Collector of Dying Breath*. It will be out in April. It features Jac L'Etoile again. As for the past, it's about Catherine de Medici's perfumer whom she brought with her from Florence to France. In the present, Jac goes to Barbizon, France where she gets involved with a woman who has collected a series of bottles that hold dying breaths. Is there or is there not, a formula by which a dying breath can be reanimated?

Henry Ford and Thomas Edison believed the soul leaves the body in your dying breath. Thomas Edison's dying breath is in his house, on display there. When I read about it, I became fascinated with this concept; namely, what would happen if you could reanimate a person through a dying breath?

Mark Rubinstein has coauthored five medical self-help books: *The First Encounter: The Beginnings in Psychotherapy*, *The Complete Book of Cosmetic Facial Surgery*, *New Choices: the Latest Options in Treating Breast Cancer*, *Heartplan: A Complete Program for Total Fitness of Heart & Mind*, and *The Growing Years: A Guide to Your Child's Emotional Development from Birth to Adolescence*, and wrote the novels *Mad Dog House*, named a Finalist for the 2012 ForeWord Reviews Book of the Year Award (Thriller & Suspense), and *Love Gone Mad*.

www.MarkRubinstein-Author.com

THE PERSECUTION OF MILDRED DUNLAP

Author: Paulette Mahurin
Page count: 204
ISBN: 978-0-9771866-1-7
Formats: Paperback, ebook
Find the author on Facebook
Star rating: 

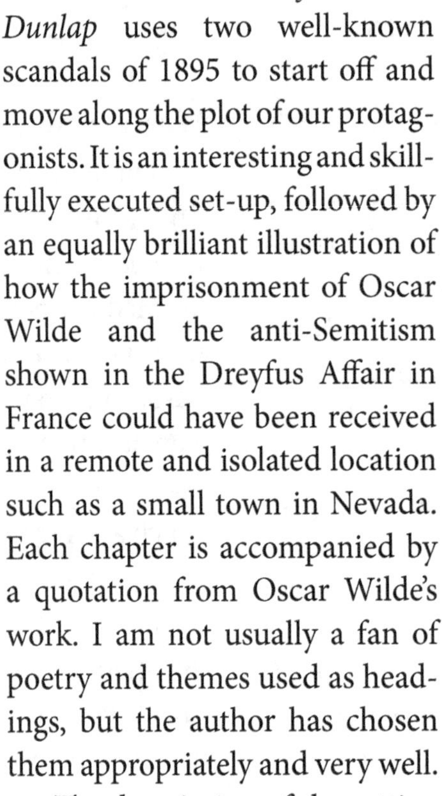

The Persecution of Mildred Dunlap uses two well-known scandals of 1895 to start off and move along the plot of our protagonists. It is an interesting and skillfully executed set-up, followed by an equally brilliant illustration of how the imprisonment of Oscar Wilde and the anti-Semitism shown in the Dreyfus Affair in France could have been received in a remote and isolated location such as a small town in Nevada. Each chapter is accompanied by a quotation from Oscar Wilde's work. I am not usually a fan of poetry and themes used as headings, but the author has chosen them appropriately and very well.

The description of the setting succeeds effortlessly with just enough detail to make it easy for us to imagine we are there with the heroes, but without overloading us with description that gets in the way of the plot. The portrayal of the times seems also very authentic and the dialogue is also very realistic and flows easily. The way the characters interact with each other is simply brilliantly done and gives the book a lively feeling. The story is much more complex and involved than the beginning and the book title seemed to imply to me – which made this an unpredictable and compulsive reading experience.

The book is an illustration of hate, intolerance and gossip in a small community and is kind and politically correct in its message. At a time when Gay Marriage proposals are being voted on all over the world and homophobia comes back into the spotlight of media attention this story is reminiscent of many of our current arguments.

At first I found it unbelievable and off-putting that some of the characters would – at that time in history – have the understanding and tolerance as the author attributes to them. Then I realized that the same ancient prejudiced views that haunt our Mildred in the book are still around in 2012.

It is a chronicle of hatred and prejudice with all its unintended and devastating consequences, and how love and friendship bring strength and healing. The book is a great piece of work on human nature and I will be recommending it to my friends.

All proceeds from this book go to a No-Kill Animal Shelter in Santa Paula Animal Rescue Center

REVIEWS BY CHRISTOPH FISCHER

INTERVIEW WITH PAULETTE MAHURIN

What was your connection or special interest in the subject matter?

The main theme of my story is intolerance, bigotry, prejudice; the labeling of another using words of hatred designed to bully, put down, change, make wrong, not accept for who they fundamentally are, their natural self that can no more be changed than a bird from flying, a dog from wagging its tail, a heart from beating. The other prevailing theme is love, the love of friends, family and intimate connections and how it is this love that surmounts hostility and brings healing. I've been working with people in the closet professionally to help them feel good about being themselves and not feeling ashamed because of a preference. The work I had done with one particular individual weighed heavily on me. This person was molested and tortured; abuse emotionally and physically and feared coming out.

I am an advocate of tolerance, the granting of another to be who they are and do what they want, providing they are not harming another by their actions. I understand the human condition and have compassion for it, the emotions we all have in common, many we want to hide or escape. I understand how hard it is to be conditioned or programmed by ones parents with a belief or ideology that goes along with belonging to a family or group, "group think", and how difficult it is to stand alone for what is right, what sits right in ones heart. I also understand why someone is in the closet and would want to stay there.

My special interest in writing this book was to give a voice to all those who have suffered intolerance, all those agonized cries in the night, alone in the dark for fear of persecution, imprisonment, being thrown into a mental institution, burned at the stake, put in a gas chamber, or simply not allowed to live a life as they chose. I wrote this story, not under the framework of hatred but love, the love of a partner, a friend for it is love that shines through the dark shadows of intolerance to help us see what we are otherwise blinded to.

When did you first have the idea for this book?

The first seed for the story came from a photo in a writing class. It was of two women huddled very close together with fearful looks on their faces wearing turn of the twentieth century garb. It screamed out to me "lesbian couple afraid of being found out."

How long did it take you to write?

Six years.

How comfortable do you feel writing about history?

If I put the time in to fact check and get the data, I felt very comfortable. I think the problem some get into with writing history is not doing the homework, being lazy. A reader picks up on these things.

How many rewrites did it take you?

Several and there were whole and part rewrites. I had three different editors and went through a different process with each along the way. The first editor was a read for flow and grammar structure. That went on a couple of years. The second one was a creative editor who read for how the story sat with her, was it believable, authentic? She is a professional screen/playwright and her input invaluable. She had me look at things like, "What does Mildred look like through Charley's eyes?" She gave me pages of questions, suggestions; things that didn't ring real for her and that rewrite took another year. The final one was with my publisher, again for flow and a line edit.

Who are your favorite authors / influences?

There are so many it is too hard to pick one. Stand out among them are Steinbeck, Dickens, Harper Lee, the classic tried and true writers. I've read so many books by known and unknown authors that I love that it is difficult to narrow it down. Things that influence me are those things that move me emotionally and stay with me, which is probably why I want to write about them because they live inside of me for some unexplained reason and in writing sometimes the answers are revealed. In this particular story it was intolerance that influenced me. In another story I'm working on it was the heroics of an ordinary couple with an extraordinary situation that brought them together in love that influenced and motivated me to want to write about them. There isn't one person, one author, that is my favorite or who influences me, rather situational things that land in my life and move me.

Bio:

Paulette Mahurin, an award-winning best selling author, is a Nurse Practitioner who lives in Ojai, California with her husband Terry and their two dogs–Max and Bella. She practices women's health in a rural clinic and writes in her spare time. She is an animal advocate and has been involved with dog rescue, along with her husband, for the past twenty-eight years. All profits from her book, The Persecution of Mildred Dunlap, are going to the Santa Paula Animal Rescue Center (the first and only no-kill shelter in Ventura County, CA).

Find the Author Online:

Goodreads:
Shelfari
Book's Blog:
Twitter
Book's Website

EMANCIPATING ALICE

Author: Ada Winder
Page count: 306
ISBN: 978-1480235090
Formats: Paperback, ebook
Find the author on Facebook and GoodReads
Star rating: ★★★★★

Short-listed for the Amazon Breakthrough Novel Award 2013

Emancipating Alice by Ada Winder is a book I have been looking forward to reading for some time and it stayed at the bottom of my pile as incentive to do less promising work. I knew from the first page onwards I was going to like this and I was right about that.

After over 30 years of marriage George dies and his widow Alice needs to come to terms with her loss and her memories. A very sentimental but incredibly well done and touching first part tells us about the first few days after the death and – in flashbacks – how the couple met and how they fell in love. Gradually we learn more about the seemingly happy and perfect family and come to realize that not all was or is well in the family relations. Thoughts of sacrifices and missed opportunities loom as the end of that particular road has arrived.

Winder writes with such an empathetic voice and great psychological understanding of her characters that I found it very hard to believe that these were not real people and Alice not Ada herself, that convincing is the writing and the heartfelt tone of Alice's voice. I found it all the more touching, yet Alice is far from the one-dimensional grief-struck widow that this review begins to make her out to be. But I must leave that all for you to explore yourself.

Part two hands the story over to George and his perspective, where we learn more about his private life and his reasons for the various choices and actions he took in his life.

This book is a piece of art; with the description of the family rows and animosities and the funeral itself this has transgressed far beyond the simple tale of a death, it has become the story of an entire family and their secrets, lies and problems. The book is sad and reflective in many parts but also fast moving and emotional in many other ways. As far as you can ever fairly compare writers to each other this is somewhat reminiscent of the writings of Lionel Shriver and Anne Tyler, two of my favorite authors but that is by no means an accusation of imitation but a huge compliment from the reviewer. "Emancipating Alice" writes honest and perceptive about human nature just as much as Shriver and Tyler do, so all three are "stealing" from the same pool of inspiration called life.

REVIEWS BY CHRISTOPH FISCHER

INTERVIEW WITH ADA WINDER

How did you come to writing in the first place?

You've probably heard this a lot by now, but writing actually came to me–very easily, very young. I was working on my first novel by the time I was nine and had produced tons of short stories and poetry before then (and continued to do so).

I think it has to do with reading early–I'd learned at the age of two and read voraciously thereafter. Plus I've always been terribly introverted; it's only natural I think for me to prefer communicating through writing.

When did you first have the idea for this book? Why this subject?

Emancipating Alice started off as two separate short story ideas, but the way the two began playing themselves out in my mind made me realize they could actually be part of the same story.

I was participating in my very first National Novel Writing Month and in the planning stage, tested out several ideas for viability. While outlining, this two-became-one project persevered–I think because one of its subplots came ready-made as a result of the merger!

How did you think of those characters?

The characters kind of populated themselves, inspired by me being a witness to some unhappy relationships. The main characters–Alice and George–showed up clearly when it was only about them as a short story. Then in planning the novel, others presented themselves–their children for example. Then of course, a few unplanned ones sort of came out of nowhere while writing, letting me know that this story was part of their story too, and for some, they ended up having a much larger part in how things played out than I imagined when they first showed up.

Do you have a favorite character in the book?

I do actually, and it ended up being one of those unplanned characters: Miriam, George's sister. She's sort of like me–a bit odd, quirky. But then again, all the women in the novel are sort of like me one way or another.

Who are your favorite authors / influences?

I read Dostoevsky's Crime and Punishment some months before I wrote Emancipating Alice and fell madly in love with his writing, the way he delved into psychology. I also read Richard Flanagan's The Sound of One Hand Clapping a few years before writing the novel and it blew my mind; it was the most beautiful, moving book I'd ever read. The author weaved in the backgrounds of its main characters–childhood events and various traumas–so that no matter how they acted, or what terrible things they did, you understood.

The way I wrote Emancipating Alice was influenced by me wanting desperately to present characters similarly–to give a hint or more as to why characters acted the way they did, why they would respond one way versus another, what affect their choices had on them. My goal was to have their actions understandable–no matter how 'bad' or 'evil,' or even banal. I can't say if I succeeded or not, but I hope I did them some justice.

I guess I'd be remiss if I didn't mention the short story: "The Yellow Wallpaper" by Charlotte Perkins Gilman–that was probably an influence as well. And I'm also a fan of Edgar Allan Poe, but I'm not sure if he got in there.

Who would play your characters in a movie?

Meryl Streep would play everyone I think–her first, multi-character movie like Eddie Murphy in The Nutty Professor.

But seriously, Meryl Streep. For Alice at least.

What is your next project and where would we be likely to hear about them?

I have short stories and novels in the works, and I will most likely post any updates on my Facebook and GoodReads page.

MR ALHOURANI'S DEAD MAN'S SPOTS

Author: DM Lee
Page count: 300 (estimated)
Formats: ebook
Find the author on GoodReads
Star rating: 

REVIEWS BY CHRISTOPH FISCHER

Mr Alhourani's Dead Man's Spots by DM Lee was an absolute treat for me. From the first page I realized that I had found a literary home for the next few hundred pages. The book is charmingly funny and entertaining, has several good plotlines, is at times sad and philosophical and leaves you with a warm and good feeling in the end.

Caretaker Annie Grimes moves from Dover to London where she gradually establishes her new and own life. She finds a bedsit, a new job and makes her first friends in the cultural melting pot that London has become. Although the story has some elements of the chick lit genre there is a lot of depth to the main character. She may be young and naïve and may remind us in some of the more sad scenes of a Bridget Jones but she ultimately has a very big and good heart and a likeable warm personality that is capable of much more than just self-pity. Her desire to help people is what gets her into trouble in the first place but the way she masters her challenges is what makes her so likeable.

Particularly great are the scenes depicting the elderly people in her care home which are written with so much understanding, respect and love for the individuals. Annie's dignified and human approach to each of them makes her a shining example to all of us who become so wrapped up in ourselves that we don't properly care for strangers anymore – as is often said about Londoners.

Annie's landlord, the Mr. Alhourani from the title, is another fantastic character. I had my reservations about him initially since he seemed portrayed as the typical Indian shop owner but I soon forgot all about it as he becomes a closer friend of our heroine and shares his unsolicited and undiplomatic advice and yet invaluable wisdom with her. He too is warm and caring and has a heart of gold and a deep side to him underneath the hard façade he has built around him. I already miss him in my own life.

The Dead Man's Spots from the title refer to his hobby of looking at the blue plaques on London buildings that honor famous people who had a connection with these houses. It brings in the element of what London as a city really is and who Londoners are – or who is and who is not a Londoner. The book brings together a variety of people – as does London – and shows how they can learn and benefit from each other, regardless of their race, religion or other beliefs.

The writing is tight and flows easily and I found myself reading much faster than I would have liked in order to make the experience last. This book is lovely and highly recommended.

INTERVIEW WITH DM LEE

How did you come to writing in the first place?

At the beginning of 2012 I decided that I would write a novel, create a story that contains strong characters, written in an entertaining manner, whilst touching on subjects that I see as being relevant to today's society. Mr Alhourani's Dead Man's Spots is the result.

What was your connection or special interest in the subject matter?

We all seek heroes. Acknowledging past success is important in helping us believe we can create a better future. I try to convey this in Mr Alhourani's character, the ability of a person to make a difference, at the same time portraying him as someone who looks for inspiration in the world around him.

History trails behind us and we move on in the name of progress. But not all progress is real progress, especially if we start to leave important elements of society behind, children, the elderly, the family unit.

When did you first have the idea for this book?

The finished story has moved a long way from the original concept. I was going to write a story based around the loneliness of one person, living in a big city, surrounded by millions. But as I developed an idea of who Annie Grimes really was, I also began to get a clearer picture of how Mr Alhourani could impact on the story, I recognized there were other elements that could add strength to the story. It was certainly an idea that evolved, even after I started writing.

Whereas, the book is based around the two main characters, I would like to think that bigger issues get brought to light, hopefully not in an over-preaching manner but in an obvious enough way for the reader to give them some thought and consideration once they've finished reading.

Who are your favorite authors / influences?

I can't honestly say I have a favorite author, people like Tony Parsons, Nick Hornby tell great stories with believable characters. Other writers like Robert Tressell manage to build a good story around a social injustice — The Ragged Trousered Philanthropists. I really felt pulled into the story in Shantaram by Gregory David Roberts, finding his characters nearly live like, especially Prabaker.

The above are just some examples, and it is probably unfair to list those when there are so many other great writers.

I probably fall more on the side of great storytelling rather great writing. I believe storytelling is the ability to capture the reader's imagination, whereas, writing is the ability to capture the right words, to create sentences that add power to the telling of a story. In the end, if I am going to ask for your time, I need to be the best storyteller and writer I can be. That's my aim.

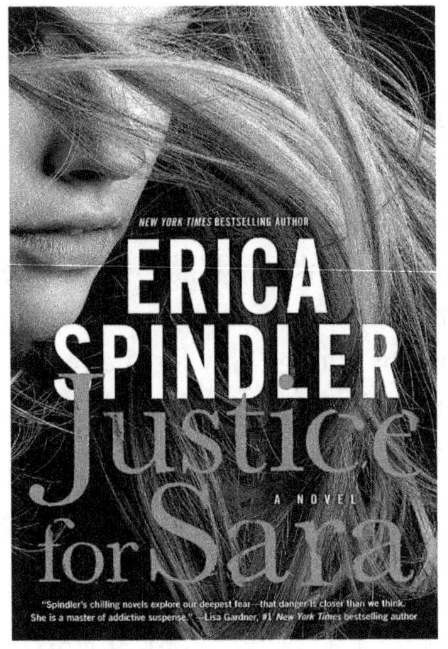

JUSTICE FOR SARA

Author: Erica Spindler
ISBN: 9781250012524
Page count: 300 (estimated)
Formats: Hardcover, Paperback, ebook, Audiobook, CD
Find the author at www.EricaSpindler.com
Star rating: ★★★★★

REVIEW BY FRAN LEWIS

OVERVIEW: Kat McCall was seventeen when her sister Sara was murdered, brutally beaten to death with a baseball bat. And as her sister lay dying inside the home they shared, Kat claimed she was locked in her bedroom, unaware of the tragedy unfolding just outside her door. Liberty Chief of Police Stephen Tanner was convinced it was Kat who carried out the crime, and so had her charged and tried. But in the case of the People of Louisiana vs. Katherine Ann McCall, Kat was found not guilty.

Ten years have passed since Kat picked up and left little Liberty, Louisiana - and the site of her sister's murder - for a fresh start on the west coast. End of story — except, despite moving more than 2,500 miles from her childhood home, Kat still receives the letters. Letters, taunting her, threatening her, and demanding she seek justice for Sara's death.

Finally prompted to move home to catch the killer no one else could and seek justice for both her and her sister, Kat snoops around and gets hot for the police chief's son, Sergeant Luke Tanner. Together the two reopen the decade-old case, reconvening the leading players: Danny Sullivan, her sister's ex-boyfriend and gambling addict; Ryan Benton, Kat's gold-digging, short-tempered ex-flame; and Bitsy Cavenaugh, Kat's jealousy-riddled childhood friend.

REVIEW: Like a roller coaster whose speed knows no bounds and a Ferris wheel that turns out of control, the lives of two young girls take a downward spiral as the roller coaster comes to a stop and the Ferris wheel halts in midair, leaving sorrow and despair in its wake.

Sara and Kat lost their parents in an accident, leaving Sara to care for her rebellious younger sister. Resentments ran high as Sara tried to be both mother and father to Kat and received nothing but hard times and grief from Kat. Life does not always go the way you want it to, and Kat's behavior towards her sister, her attitude, and one argument would change the course of both of their lives forever.

Waking up one morning in June and getting ready for school, little did she know that her day would not go as planned. Finding her sister, Sara, beaten to death with a bat by what police say was definitely an assailant she knew, would terrify most and cause them to break down and cry. But, Kat was tough, hard-nosed, and at seventeen, although thinking she was streetwise and smart, in reality was just plain naïve.

Katherine McCall has lived the last ten years with a black cloud hanging over her head. At seventeen she, as many teens do, defied those in charge, rebelled against rules, and often got herself into trouble, and could not understand why she had to pay the consequences. The story opens with Katherine returning to her hometown after those ten years. The story flashes back and forth between the present and the days before and after the murder. We meet Sara as she tried her best to discipline Kat and encourage her to choose the right friends, and learned just what happens when you try to tame a teen. Kat's voice comes through as being tough, hardcore, rude and unfeeling when dealing with her sister. Resenting the fact that if she did not adhere to Sara's rules Kat would not get her inheritance, she was forced to go along with her.

Kat found her way into the arms of a young man named Ryan, who everyone else could tell was only in the relationship for the money she would inherit that would put him on easy street. Their romance might have been hot and heavy, but his motives were definitely suspect. Next, we meet the police chief that questioned her at the time of her sister's death. Kat remained calm to a point, almost as if she did not realize that what she saw was real and that her sister was really gone. At times as she was questioned, the reader might think that she did not process what was being asked, and although her cousin Jeremy, her lawyer, was present, the events and the end result would make her the prime suspect in her sister's murder.

Forwarding to the present, we meet Sergeant Luke Tanner, who took over for his father the chief of police, who is on medical leave and whose resentment towards Kat has not changed after ten years. The evidence was in, the witnesses questioned, and a jury of her peers had acquitted her of her sister's murder. Coming back to Liberty, the town where the murder took place, took guts you might say. Kat was determined to find out who murdered her sister and why, and establish herself in the town as a business owner of a bakery and bread store. But, there was much more as we hear about Sara's boyfriend Danny and the police interview with him.

Ryan, the young man that Kat was dating at the time, came face to face with her in the present, and the confrontation brought harsh words, bad memories, and one young man who thought that the world owed him something. While talking with him Kat even stated that she thought he might be the one who killed her sister. But, where did the bat come from that was used to murder her, and why would someone want her dead?

The reception she received from most of the people was cold and calculated. No one wanted her around, and everyone pointed fingers at her for the murder. The police had never looked for a second suspect, and even in the present everyone seemed to see a huge guilty sign on her chest. No one was willing to give her a chance, and few would. Then she met Danny, her sister's boyfriend, in the present and found that he agreed with the jury's verdict. But why?

Words are sometimes more powerful than force, and Kat's would come back to haunt her for a long time. As the author relates each character's account of the night of the murder or days before or after, we get to understand why some thought Kat might have wanted her sister dead. Sara had wanted to send her to boarding school because of the company she kept, her sneaking out of her room, and constantly telling lies. Hearing Chief Tanner question her, we realize that he left many stones unturned, and as a result missed important evidence that might have solved Wally Clark's murder and Sara's too. But, there was much more, and we get to know Ryan in the present and Kat's best friend and now Ryan's future wife, Bitsy, whose agenda is quite different and whose account we learn is quite enlightening. The author brilliantly flashes back to the night of the murder, and we hear Danny's account of where he was and why he was angry with Sara, and learn more about his gambling problems.

Throughout the novel we also see the tension between Luke and his father as we learn about his brother's death, the reason his father became so distant, and the end result that might tear them both apart. Secrets, lies, and deceptions emerge about the night Sara and Wally were both killed and families that would forever change. But, Kat would not let go and even though many things happened to her and we learn more about her relationship with her cousin Jeremy and the resentment his wife feels for her, she forged ahead, spoke to Ms. Bell, and the end result will surprise the reader. Questions, no answers, one man that did not see past Kat as the suspect, and two murders that might never be solved.

Within the framework of the story is an underlying romance between Kat and Luke. Taken with her and hoping to get to know her better, Luke believed in her innocence, protected her when things happened that let her know that the killer was still out there, and decided to reopen her case. But, there was a second murder that night of a police officer, and some think the two were linked. Someone was stalking Kat with letters for over ten years, hoping she would back off, that they could create fear within her and she would hopefully disappear. But, rather than become a shrinking violet she had kept the letters and now showed them to Luke. But the vandalism to her car and the fire in her home proved that someone still wanted her out of the way.

The author flashes back to two days after the murder, and we hear the voice of Iris Bell, her neighbor, recounting her thoughts about Kat and her relationship with Sara. The author does this in timeline fashion so expertly that the reader takes the journey back in time with the characters as we get to understand their possible motives for murdering Sara, and who the other suspects might be. The author also allows readers to hear the voice of the lawyer, understand his relationship to both Sara and Kat, and then brings us to the present where he decides to run for state senator.

Kat harbored resentment and fear of what might happen to her as she witnessed her house burning, stated her views on Sara's boyfriend Danny, and was hiding secrets that had yet to be revealed. Remembering her sister had a journal and that no one could find it sent Kat to a storage locker to retrieve the items from their past, but the fire took it all.

When Kat receives another letter from who the author calls The Fan, stating "What about justice for Sara?" the reader wonders if this question is two fold: When will justice vindicate Kat, or when will the real killer be found? It was the tenth anniversary of her death, and someone wanted it to be the last one Kat would remember.

When Kat confronted her fears she lashed out at Luke and made some damaging accusations that might have hindered their friendship. After finding her way back to her cousin's house after the fire, she decided to take another detour and return to the scene, finding someone lurking in the dark. The end result would bring in a suspect, but was he The Fan or the killer? As Luke tried to decipher what was going on and backtracked the two murders, would he find a link? Why did Sara's boyfriend hate her uncle?

With an explosive ending, when the truth is revealed you just won't believe who killed Sara. Lies, greed, betrayals, deceit, and a town that would never forget the true meaning of *Justice For Sara.*

ABOUT ERICA SPINDLER

Catching a summer cold changed Erica Spindler's life forever.

Up until that fateful malady, Erica planned on being an artist. She had studied for that profession, earning both a BFA and MFA in the visual arts. Then in June of 1982, she stopped at a local drugstore to pick up cold tablets and tissues; the cashier dropped a free romance novel into her bag. She hadn't read a romance in years but once home, with nothing to do but sniffle and watch daytime TV, she picked that romance up — and was immediately hooked. For the next six months she read every romance she could get her hands on. Sometime during those months, she decided to try to write one herself.

The moment she put pen to paper, Erica knew she had found her true calling. Since that day, Erica has published more than twenty novels. Her titles have been published all over the world and *Red* was turned into both a wildly popular graphic novel and daytime drama in Japan. Critics have dubbed her stories as "thrill-packed, page turners, white knuckle rides, and edge-of-your-seat whodunits."

Erica is a *USA TODAY, New York Times* and Amazon.com bestseller. In 2002, her novel *Bone Cold* won the prestigious Daphne du Maurier Award for excellence. An RWA honor roll member, she received a Kiss of Death award for her novel *Forbidden Fruit* and is a three-time RITA award finalist. In 1999 *Publishers Weekly* awarded the audio version of her novel *Shocking Pink* a Listen-Up award, naming it one of the best audio mystery books of 1998.

Erica and her husband — a man she describes as funny, handsome and way too sassy — met in art school and have been together ever since. They have two sons, born nine and a half years apart. Erica makes her home in the New Orleans area, although she originally hailed from Illinois.

Erica came to her present home in much the same way she came to writing — fate intervened. She and her husband, then college students, traveled to New Orleans to see the King Tut exhibit at the New Orleans Museum of Art. Without advance tickets, they had a choice: wait in line all day or spend the day sightseeing. They chose the latter and fell head-over-heels in love with the city.

Erica is currently at work on her next thriller for St. Martin's Press.

AUTHOR OF THE MONTH

TESS GERRITSEN: FROM MD TO AUTHOR

International bestselling author Tess Gerritsen took an unusual route to a writing career. A graduate of Stanford University, Tess went on to medical school at the University of California, San Francisco, where she was awarded her M.D.

While on maternity leave from her work as a physician, she began to write fiction. In 1987, her first novel was published. Eight more romantic suspense novels followed Call After Midnight, a romantic thriller. She also wrote a screenplay, *Adrift*, which aired as a 1993 CBS Movie of the Week starring Kate Jackson.

Tess's first medical thriller, **Harvest**, was released in hardcover in 1996, and it marked her debut on the New York Times bestseller list. Her suspense novels since then have been: **Life Support** (1997), **Bloodstream** (1998), **Gravity** (1999), **The Surgeon** (2001), **The Apprentice** (2002), **The Sinner** (2003), **Body Double** (2004), **Vanish** (2005), **The Mephisto Club** (2006), **The Bone Garden** (2007), **The Keepsake** (2008; UK title: Keeping the Dead), **Ice Cold** (2010; UK title: The Killing Place), **The Silent Girl** (2011), and **Last To Die** (August 2012.) Her books have been published in forty countries, and more than 25 million copies have been sold around the world.

Her books have been top-3 bestsellers in the United States and abroad. She has won both the Nero Wolfe Award (for Vanish) and the Rita Award (for The Surgeon). Critics around the world have praised her novels as "Pulse-pounding fun" (Philadelphia Inquirer), "Scary and brilliant" (Toronto Globe and Mail), and "Polished, riveting prose" (Chicago Tribune). Publisher Weekly has dubbed her the "medical suspense queen".

INTERVIEW WITH TESS GERRITSEN

MJ Magazine would like to welcome *New York Times* Best Selling Author: Tess Gerritsen: Here is a special interview that I did with this outstanding author:

1. **Tell everyone about your background and how you incorporate it in your novels.**

I'm a medical doctor (practiced only about five years), an enthusiastic traveler, and very interested in science. I use all these facets of my own life in the books. It's the medical background that really set my books apart, I think, first with my medical thrillers, and later with my medical examiner character, Maura isles. But everything in your life is grist for the mill. I used my interest in archaeology in *The Keepsake,* my Asian heritage in *The Silent Girl* and my fascination with creepy news stories in *Vanish.* Above all, a writer must be curious.

2. **Using your knowledge of medicine, how do you incorporate it in each of your novels? Which character/characters would you say would mirror you?**

Maura Isles is an M.D., so the way she thinks, the way she approaches a cadaver, is very much told from a doctor's point of view. I'm not sure I'd be able to do it as realistically if I weren't medically trained. I often slip in odd information about unusual diseases or causes of death or poisons. I also find that medical topics end up being vital to the plot (e.g. leprosy plays a role in *The Sinner.*) As for which character is me — it's definitely Maura.

3. **When creating a character in a series how do you manage to increase the suspense, help the character grow in order to keep reader interest?**

I really don't plan anything out, and the characters seemed to develop themselves. In truth, neither Jane nor Maura were designed to be series characters. I thought, when they first appeared on the page, that they'd last one book and then I'd move on to something else. But they had quirks — introduced entirely subconsciously on my part — that made me wonder what happened next to them. Jane was smart and determined but very plain looking, and I wanted to see if she'd find a man who'd love her. Maura was mysterious and hard to read, and I wanted to find out what made her tick. A lot of character development is allowing your subconscious to take over and imbue these blank slates with the details that make them real.

4. **What are Jane's strongest character traits? How does she manage to withstand the way she is treated at first when becoming a detective? Why do her superiors resent her?**

She's a fighter and survivor — that's the one thing I knew about her. I also knew that she had to fight hard for respect, because not only is she a woman in a man's profession, she's also not particularly beautiful. She considers herself an outsider, and that's something I identified with very strongly because it defines my own life as well. So despite the roadblocks put in her way, you know that Jane will always find a way to get past them. Why do her superiors resent her? Because she's abrasive and tells you what she thinks. She's not one for niceties, and not everyone appreciates that honesty.

5. **Moira is the ME: she and Jane formed a great bond, yet they are so different. How do they manage that?**

Their bond is formed through mutual respect, and that's really what makes that friendship tick. They both trust each other to do the best job possible, and through trust they've become friends. They're not the kind of women who would naturally be friends. Jane's from a blue-collar background and Maura is very much from an educated family. Yet they know that there's no one better in a pinch than each other.

6. Why do you add a new character in each novel, and which ones have had reoccurring appearances and why?

It's always hit or miss. Sometimes I'll add a new character and think, *That's it. I'm done with him or her.* But then a book or two later, I realize I miss that character and want to see him back. Korsak, for instance — I love that guy, as unattractive as he is. There are characters who just grow on you and never leave you.

7. When creating the plot for a new novel, do you prepare a plot outline, chapter outline, or create the dialogue and role for each character then blend it all together?

No outline, very little plot, and certainly I don't have any game plan for the characters. I just put them on the page and let them do the talking. My first drafts are a mess because I'm very much feeling my way through the story.

8. What was your first title? What was it and how did your writing change? Will you write another stand alone like Bone Garden?

My first books were romances, and my first officially published novel was *Call After Midnight,* which I am still very proud of. At the time I wrote it, I was reading and enjoying romances, and it was the genre I loved to write as well. As for what I'll write in the future, I am currently under contract to write two more Rizzoli & Isles books. But I would love to do other stand-alones as well.

9. If you could add another strong female character to your Rizolli and Isles series, where do you see this person fitting in and what role would she play?

I haven't thought of any other strong continuing female characters, although I do think that Jane's mother will have a large role in an upcoming book.

10. Will Gabriel ever be the main character of one of your novels?

No plans at this time.

11. What are the most important elements that go into writing a novel?

I need interesting characters most of all. There can be a terrific premise and a wham-bam plot, but if I don't connect with the characters, then I don't care to write the book.

12. What made you decide to change careers and write?

I wanted to be a writer first; medicine was just a detour I took to be able to pay the bills. So when I started writing (during maternity leave) it was really a return to my first love.

13. When you are stumped and need to take a break...when the plot line or characters are not cooperating...how do you deal with writer's block?

I go for a long drive. Or I lie on the couch and stare at the ceiling. Most of all, I give myself permission to walk away from the book for a few days or weeks to solve whatever plot problem I'm struggling with.

14. How do you decide on the plot of your book?

I start with a premise that really affects me emotionally. Either it's upsetting or shocking or terrifying. Then I ask, "What happens next?" Writing the book is about answering that question. *Vanish,* for instance, started with the premise of a woman waking up in a body bag. Why was she mistaken for dead? Who is she? What does she do next? The story just kept moving forward with more and more complications, but it all began with the terrifying premise of being mistaken for dead.

15. If you could be a character in any author's novel, which author, what novel, and what character?

I'd like to be Hermione Granger! Who would+n't want to be the most impressive witch of her time?

16. If you could work with any detective, real or fictional, who would it be and how would you incorporate that person into your novel?

Sherlock Holmes. I'd like him to teach me more about the powers of observation!

17. Which character is most like you and why?

Maura Isles. We're both introverts who believe in the power of science.

18. What is your next project and when will readers be able to get your next title?

I'm working on a Rizzoli & Isles novel, where the mystery is intimately connected with the fate of a doomed safari party in Africa. Having a great time with this one! But I haven't figured out a title yet.

19. Where can readers learn more about you?

They can always follow me on Twitter or on Facebook!

20. What is your website?

www.TessGerritsen.com

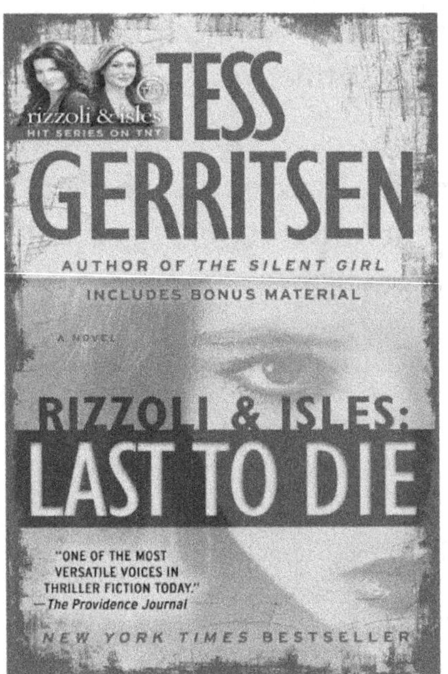

LAST TO DIE

Author: Tess Gerritsen
Page count: 352
ISBN: 978-0553825640
Formats: hardcover, paperback, ebook, MP3, audio book
Find the author: www.TessGerritsen.com
Star rating: 

REVIEW BY FRAN LEWIS

Monsters are born everyday and of course they don't deserve to live. Those that prey on other people justify their actions within their own minds. Some find it is their calling to go after these monsters as did the person referred to as Icarus in the prologue of this book.

Thirteen-year-old Claire Ward was supposed to have a date with death. So, how did she escape? Living with her foster parents, rebellious, and resenting the restrictions placed on her, Claire looked for a way to release her tensions and frustrations but at what cost? Claire decides to take a leap of faith and jump from her window to freedom, hoping she wouldn't get caught. But, something happens to change her destiny and the lives of many others before all was said and done that night.

Meeting her friends at midnight was her first mistake, and getting caught her second. It was a mistake not just for her but also for her foster parents, Bob and Barbara Buckley. Claire finally gets into the car that Barbara is driving, and what happens next will definitely make the reader pause for thought. Headlights hurtled in their direction, and end the lives of her foster parents. A strange woman says Claire's name, and she had no choice but to go with her.

Fourteen-year-old Will Yablonksi loves to hunt for aliens, and lives with his aunt and uncle on their farm. His father has passed away and Will's goal is to find a comet and name it after him, Comet Neil Yablonski. Will loves to look up into the sky and enjoys going out with his Uncle Brian to see what the night sky offers. One evening, he goes out alone to the field behind his aunt and uncle's farmhouse. An explosion comes from out of nowhere and catches his attention — he thought he'd found the comet, but realizes he did not. Hoping to save his aunt and uncle from the blazing farmhouse, the same woman Claire went with appears and takes him to safety. Who she is and why these things are happening remains a mystery.

Jane and her mother were discussing what she would wear to her upcoming wedding. Jane hated pink but her mother was dead set on her wearing a pink gown. But, this was just the tip of the iceberg for that day before meeting her close friend, ME Maura Isles at a gruesome murder scene witnessing a sight that would haunt most and terrify others. When viewing the bodies they seem to want to tell their own story.

When Jane finally meets Teddy, she could tell he was traumatized, but for some reason he started to trust her and explained what he saw, which was not much. Losing his glasses made it difficult for him to focus on anything more than the killer's black shoes. The fear that enveloped him made it so he couldn't come out from under his bed until the next day. Midnight seemed to be the link to all three murders, as they all occurred around that time.

Darren Crowe seemed hardnosed, unfeeling, and determined to solve the case at all costs. But, Jane was strong and straightforward, and handled his remarks quite boldly as the rest of the team just listened. She hoped to find a link between the murder of Teddy's birth parents two years before and the recent murder of his foster parents. The boy was fragile and scared, and only Jane provided any kind of hope for his safety.

Did he fear her help? Would she be next to die if she helped him? What was the link between the two murders? Why were the foster kids left alive in all three cases? These questions are a long way from being answered as the author once again allows the reader to hear from the narrator. He is hoping to catch the man he calls Icarus, whose lifestyle mirrors that of a rich Italian Don, and whose young son stared him right in the eye.

Maura visited the places where all of the foster children were now living. Julian Perkins, the young man who saved her life and who had the uncanny ability to see things that most didn't, came with her. Sheltered from harm, these students lived in an amazing structure along with Lily and Anthony, whose pasts were scarred and whose hopes for the future of these students were high. Claire and Will were hoping to find a place for themselves in this odd world filled with students that were anything but ordinary.

Maura feared that something in the school was not right. Each foster child was a lone survivor of a mass murder, and each teen had nowhere to turn and felt alienated and alone. Maura voiced her concerns about what she realized was going on at the school and their objectives for the students. As she contemplated pulling Julian out, another child was whisked in.

Teddy Clock's safety was once again in jeopardy when someone invaded his home. Could all three children's situations be linked to the same killer? What was the motive? What was the killer's mission?

Once again, author Tess Gerristen brings the reader front and center into the world of private schools, forensic medicine, and police work. The story is compelling as the detective and ME refuse to give up on their quest to find the killer before someone else is *The Last One To Die*. Trust, loyalty, friendship, and hope are at the core of this story.

This is Tess at her best, with an ending that will leave you wondering what is next for Jane and Maura and where the next case will take them.

FEATURED NEW AUTHOR

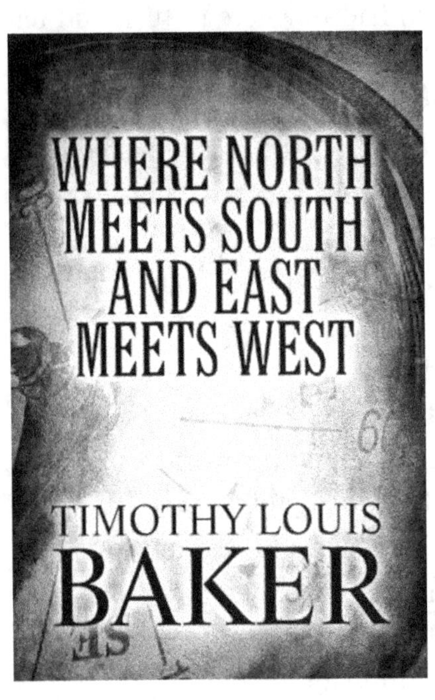

WHERE NORTH MEETS SOUTH AND EAST MEETS WEST

Author: Timothy Louis Baker
Page count: 176
ISBN: 978-1448919734
Formats: Paperback
Star rating: 

REVIEW BY FRAN LEWIS

Memories are powerful and creating a memoir that allows readers to relive these moments with you quite compelling. Timothy allowing readers to understand his early years, the pride he took in helping his father on his farm, and knowing that he made difference envelopes readers from the start. We visit his farm, help him plant the sweet corn and the soybeans, learn about his ability to drive a tractor, and find his way to making a difference.

Throughout the memoir you hear the voice of the author explain his actions, relate his missteps, and hopefully help others. Getting his driver's license, totally his car, and even using drugs led Timothy down many paths, and not all in the right direction. Hoping to help others, not making excuses for his inactions or actions, author Timothy Louis Baker hits the reader hard with the facts that will make you wonder just how he managed to survive.

Reading about life on a farm and its operation was quite interesting. Finding his way to help his parents and yet having fun with his friends proved that within his heart and spirit he was a good and kind person. Although he states that he missed much of the last two years of his high school classes, some things that he learned in order to survive and help on the farm came from hands on experience and could not be learned in the classroom, although school is important and an education invaluable.

After using hard drugs, smoking marijuana, and really enjoying the high and the scent, Timothy found that he needed harder drugs such as cocaine, LSD, and crystal meth. This makes the reader wonder how his body was able to tolerate so much without crying for help. Hitchhiking through many states, meeting some interesting people, and placing himself in tenuous situations that most would find difficult to deal with and others might even cower from, Timothy seemed able to weather many storms.

Getting in trouble with the law for stealing, robbing, drive by shootings, and using drugs did not seem to deter him from continuing his spree of dangerous actions that might lead to more serious charges. Stealing gas and his father's motorcycle, then placing him in dangerous situations while driving, something kept his going in this direction. It was almost as if he was trying to see how far he could go before someone finally stopped him or took an interest in him and curbed his appetite for drugs.

Working in a circus and describing his jobs, he relates how he broke into buildings and a candy shack to get the things needed to smoke pot, which led him back to court with a buddy, and more warrants for his arrest. You might say his life was always on the run and he seemed to be acting like a daredevil, hoping to not get caught; or maybe he hoped someone would finally stop him.

Every step of the way it seemed that Timothy was trying to find his place in this world, understand and analyze the events both positive and negative that were happening to him, and at several times thought that the police and others were out to hurt him. Not sure of the outcomes at times and in certain situations led the author to feel that he had either some psychic connection that helped him to forestall events that were about to unfold and prevent them from happening, or a keen sixth sense that kept him alive.

At times he sounds — as this memoir is related in narrative form in the author's own voice — as if he was bent on a life filled with mystery, the unknown, and hope, yet at others it almost feels like he was headed for destruction. His loyalty to his parents, the knowledge that his father needed him on the farm to do seasonal work, and his spirit of adventure and curiosity kept him centered most of the time. He loved to explore the woods and other places to find out what more there was in the world and what he could learn from it.

Living off the land and fending for he gave him a strong sense of independence and freed him of the chains of confinement most have. Living by his own rules and mores at times would benefit him and at others get him in trouble with local authorities or other law enforcement figures. But, the strength within him and his drive to succeed on his own comes through in every word and page within this memoir that takes readers in all four compass directions: North, South, East and West.

The author relates his feelings about Heaven and his experiences related to Heaven where there would be no floods, earthquakes, or natural disasters. He even includes his paranormal experiences and feels at times that he is caught in between two time periods, or as he relates, a time warp. He feels that there is a black warlock that has been intertwined within his thoughts, changing events and even hoping to give his own perspective on Timothy's life.

Stressing how he broke the law, went to jail many times yet did not really learn his lesson strikes an important chord for young teens to know that jail is not a fun experience, drinking and driving is dangerous, plus using hard core drugs can definitely impair your mind. Homeless centers, jail cells, hitchhiking, living off the land, on the street, and struggling to survive, Timothy Louis Baker presents a harsh look at the realities of life when someone plays daredevil with the outcome.

You will learn more about the warlock and his demise. Marriage, a child, and finally being asked to work with law enforcement to take drug dealers down … this is one interesting memoir told by the author in his own words, giving the world the cold hard truth about his life.

The final chapters summarize his dealings about other law enforcement agencies, being in a mental hospital, his paranormal experiences, time warp experiences, and much more that explains his views and experiences as he sees them. His father witnessed some of his paranormal experiences that you need to read about for yourself and form your own opinion.

One thing for sure is that Timothy carved out his life in his own way, and created the incidents that happened to him by himself, and he takes ownership of his choices. Read this straightforward memoir of this man's life and take the trip from North to South, East and West and join him as he lives his life his way.

ABOUT TIMOTHY LOUIS BAKER

Timothy Louis Baker began writing seriously in 2000. He has written seven books, exclusively on topics that he was either knowledgeable about from his personal life or from stories he heard from other individuals he came into personal contact with. His books include: *Where North Meets South and East Meets West, Fantastic Florida Fun, Crime and Drugs on Trip City Street, Wilderness Generations, An Experience Heaven Sent, American Lives Past, Autobiography of an Adventuresome Life, The Orange Groves,* and *My Life's History in Poetry. Visit his website at http://sbpra.com/authortimothybaker/*

BOOKS DEALING WITH ISSUES

NOVEMBER SPECIAL FOCUS: SPECIAL NEEDS CHILDREN: AUTISM

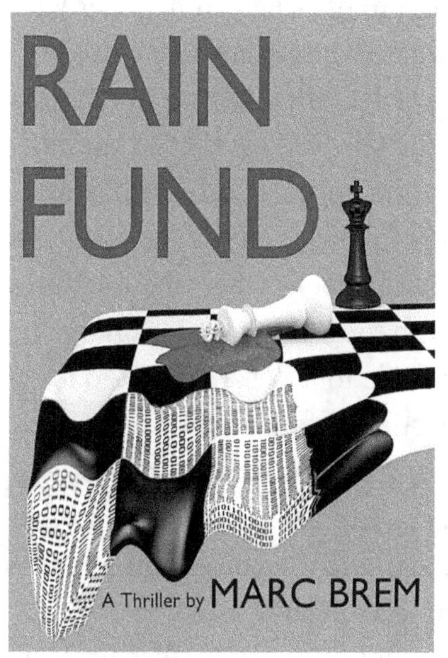

RAIN FUND
Author: Marc Brem
Page count: 356
ISBN: 978-0956990792
Formats: Paperback, ebook

REVIEW BY FRAN LEWIS

Can autistic savants be material in creating the trend for a Rain Fund? Can their knowledge and their persistence in trying to complete a goal, sticking to it, and blocking out the outside world is their link to success? Autistic savants are highly intelligent, yet as we learn more about Timothy, a young man who works for *Rain Fund,* the title of this novel, we find out more about a man named Olivier Van Dijk.

This man runs the Rain Fund, founded it, and has created a situation that would enlist and train autistic savants, and base trading decisions on what they think and do regarding this leading hedge fund called the Rain Fund. Can these autistic people actually control the trend of a hedge fund? What about those who are dyslexic or have ADD?

From the start we learn the meaning of Rain Fund, how it is compared to a Ponzi scheme, and we listen to the voice of the man who created it along with his best friend Alex to learn more about what some might say is a get rich scheme.

Rain Fund is a thriller that asks many questions from the start: Can a person with learning difficulties be the link to more successful performance? Could they actually predict the trend for a hedge fund? These people are noted to have unbelievable memories and capabilities in math and memory that might far surpass that of people without any deficiencies.

The author from the start even refers to the movie *Rain Man* with Tom Cruise and Dustin Hoffman as a reference for what he is trying to relate to readers. Listen to the voice of Olivier and the banter between him and Alex to learn the underlying truth about this Rain Fund. Meet the rest of the characters, the head of security, and learn more about Alex and the Prometheus Foundation, where he holds many meetings.

He is about to learn more about Dr. Laura Wheelan, but not before we learn that someone is following Olivier and wants him eliminated. We also hear the voice of someone connected to the fund, who manages to eliminate someone close to Olivier without any detection, and who is what you might say a psychopathic head of the Latvian Mafia. He is only concerned about the Fund and making sure that he makes billions, and the chills you get when you hear him speak allows the reader to know that he is more than just dangerous and that someone close to Olivier is betraying him.

One killer who seems to want to eliminate bankers whose reputations are shady and who have been in the news commits several murders. But, let's not forget our autistic savants who are referred to as numbers, not by names, and who provide the intelligence to help the fund grow. So, who is number 3 and why are they concerned about this subject and patient? Why did Timothy get so upset when all of the numbers and colors that he liked to play with, plus the shapes, seemed to be gobbled up by a black thing that was taking over his patterns? Could this be a virus or a cyber attack?

What we learn next is most compelling as the author shares many definitions with the reader, such as whistler blower, how they are paid, where the rewards come from, and why the FBI enlisted the help of Joshua Appleseed to infiltrate the Fund, find out information about money laundering, and hopefully bring down the people that are running it. Who is behind it? The author reveals the mob, but what is the money being used for? Joshua is concerned about the safety and welfare of his son Tom, who works for the Fund, his role in helping to predict financial trends. The author also explains the many different definitions of "autistic savant," and describes how they can and cannot interact with other people. So, can these highly intelligent people work in this Fund and help shield the world from its real purpose? Will Olivier open his eyes to the corruption and life going on right in front of him, or is he a part of it?

As the FBI convinces Appleseed to be their eyes and ears, will he be able to uncover what is going on there, learn the financial markets on the autistic chart, learn more about the mob's involvement and who is following him every step of the way even before he becomes a part of the Fund himself? And what does China have to do with this? Who is going around killing bankers and stuffing playing cards into their mouths?

Going to his friend Jack's memorial service should not have proved dangerous, but Olivier, in his hope to bring some information to his wife and help her with certain things, arrives at this house just when two burglars begin searching Jack's office, but no one knows why. The end result for Olivier is a visit to the hospital, interrogation by the police, and his mind wondering why the press is following him. One relentless reporter will learn what happens when she interferes with those involved with the Fund, as questioning one of its IT men proved futile too. We are about to learn more about the connection of foreign intelligence services, whose goal is to infiltrate their computer system and create a cyber-ware using viruses and other means. So, what was making the colors and patterns turn black on Number 3's screen?

Rain Fund, this highly technical thriller by Marc Brem, introduces the reader to what happens when cyber-wars are being waged even as we speak, and how the US will countermand these attempts, most notably with Iran and in this case even China or other countries. Things start to heat up and the roles that some are playing come to light quite openly as Joshua and Laura find themselves in a difficult situation. The truth behind why they are at the Fund is revealed, and the hopes of learning more about the mathematical progressions and the trends will have to come from Jack's research and not from what Joshua could find. One reporter is now a casualty, Jack's death might be investigated, and Olivier is on the run from the police.

Betrayals, lies, deceit ... things are not always what they seem. When the entire scheme is brought to light and Olivier has to face some harsh realities, he and Laura team up to find the answers. But what they learn, what happens, and the chain of events will change more than just the complexion of the Rain Fund, the patients, and the truth behind what is really going down and why. Getting rich is the prime reason, but who is running the show? Just how far will the mob go to control the Fund? Just who can be trusted and who will pay as a result of the ultimate betrayal?

When the reality of what happened and what was placed within the computers of the foundation is revealed, only one person can find out just how to dismantle it, and hopefully do more than just save the day. The compound is infiltrated, the cameras and phones disconnected, and one young nineteen year old autistic savant has his hands on the pulse and knows what to do, but will it be in time? A virus so deadly was placed within the hardware of his system, undetected by experts, yet to Tom it was so visible it shined right through.

Characters that are well defined and who many can identify with, and research evident in dealing with special needs young adults, this educator, who worked with students with reading and learning disabilities, found this novel and the information a great resource for those who want to understand how autistic savants can be integrated into society and prove quite productive.

One psychopathic Latvian Mafia Boss, one Chinese Master-Spy, one cyber conspiracy, and one author who weaves a plot so intricate, so complex, and so frightening that this reviewer read this fast paced thriller in less than two hours. I also learned something about computer hacking, viruses, and the world of espionage, and wonder what author Marc Brem has in store for Olivier, Laura, and Joshua. Can they stop what these men want to do before more lives are lost? Will they catch the assassin before she strikes again? Who is behind the computer virus and what was this about…the Fund, money, or something else? Just what is Olivier's ingenious plan, created by our talented author, to stop these people right where it hurts and provide the end to their deadly games? Throughout the novel we hear the voice of Oliver, our narrator, and many of the other characters whose thoughts are revealed to the reader in order to understand what might and will happen next. But, the ending will definitely surprise you as the twists, turns, and definitely the unexpected will alert readers that somewhere out there someone just might want to take care of Olivier because vengeance and revenge are sweet. As Olivier, his friend who manages his money, and others enjoy a challenging game of chess along with Aivars, our mob leader, whose past is revealed throughout the novel, let me leave you with this final thought: Checkmate: But is the game over? Who wins? Read the novel and you decide!

DELLANI OAKES INTERVIEWS WENDY, WHOSE SON HAS AUTISM SPECTRUM DISORDER AND WILSON'S SYNDROME

Many of us, myself included, know very little about Autism and it's different aspects. What can you tell us to clarify it?

For me, the best way to sum up autism is that of the rainbow. Just as you have the spectrum of colors, you have the spectrum of abilities in each individual. As the colors in a spectrum go from dark to light, you have abilities that go from low to high functioning. lol I hope that makes sense!

How has your son's disability impacted your life?

Many years ago, my eldest brother said to me, "Maybe it would have better if he had died at birth. Look at all he takes from you." I replied, "Nnooo — look at all he GIVES me." My son has taught me patience, respect, unconditional love, courage … the strength to fight seemingly endless battles (all for his well being). After all is said and done, the biggest impact my son has made on my life is that he has shown me things that we neuro-typical people often take for granted. There's an old saying that says we should stop and smell the roses. But do we really? Individuals with autism or other cognitive/developmental issues actually do that. I guess unconditional love sums it up best. Me for him and vice versa.

Is Autism a disease, condition, and syndrome?

Autism is actually considered to be a disorder of neurological development. It can affect speech, cognitive, developmental, motor skills, and social behaviors.

What questions do you wish people WOULD ask you?

Can we help you with anything? There are a ton of things that I as a single parent need help with, from housework to respite care. Especially respite care. We have very little if any in the area where we live. It would also be nice for someone to just stop by and say, "Hi." (laughing) We don't get company.

What questions to you wish people *would not* ask you?

I've had many, many snide comments made. Someone asked me if I'd like some duct tape for RJ because he was making noise in the bathroom. A lot of people have commented that I should "institutionalize" him. But it isn't so much the spoken words that hurt, as it is the behaviors of those that don't understand, and don't want to. Individuals with autism are not contagious. They don't have leprosy. They are human beings and deserve to be accepted just as any other individual does. That hurts the most - when other parents pull their children away for your child in a line, or don't allow them to talk to you.

How can schools help meet the needs of these children?

Hmmm. Educational institutions have something in place for all "special needs" children called an IEP. That stands for Individualized Education Program. IEPs clarify where is child is at cognitively and developmentally, and set goals that in the school setting that will help the child progress. Each child learns on an individual level. While an IEP does benefit our children's education, I personally feel that the IEP should have more input from parents. Educators and teachers would not be where they are without many years of schooling. Although I have some college background, I don't have the teaching courses. I guess the best way to explain it is that while a teacher is "book smart", a parent is "street" smart. We as parents walk the walk and talk the talk of autism 24/7. Most educators can go home at night and put the "job" on the shelf.

When an IEP is done for a child, it creates the child's "team", which consists of teachers, therapists and the parents, possibly a social caseworker for the child. From my personal experience, the team should work together – not against each other.

Where can parents go to find help for their Autistic children?

I call it "cold calling". I will call agencies geared towards those with autism. If I can't find the answer there, I'll comment, "Thank you. Do you know who I could call?" Thus, you will possibly gain more numbers to call. We must be proactive in finding resources – they won't come to us. I have contacted such places as our county social services department, sheriff's department, salvation army, councils on aging – the list goes on. Other parents are an excellent resource and support network. The web is an excellent resource also.

I want to ask questions about Autism, but not offend someone with an Autistic child. What do I say so I am showing my genuine desire to learn, but won't sound like a smarmy, pseudo-intellectual, hypocritical, suck-up?

As parents of special needs children, I think it becomes a natural thing to recognize who is sincere and who is being hypocritical. When someone does approach me, it's much nicer to hear questioning as to why he does something this way, or does your child have a disability, rather than plain old "What's *wrong* with him?"

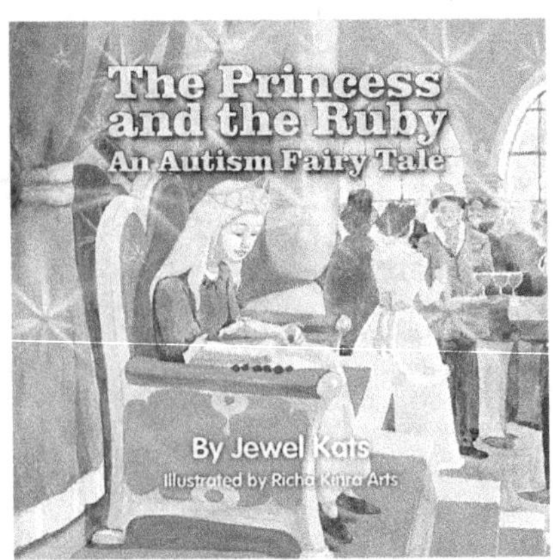

THE PRINCESS AND THE RUBY: AN AUTISM FAIRY TALE

Author: Jewel Kats
Illustrator: Richa Kinra Arts
Page count: 42
ISBN: 978-1-61599-176-1
Formats: Hardcover, Paperback, ebook
Find the author: www.JewelKats.com

REVIEW BY FRAN LEWIS

The snow is falling hard and the world is covered in a white blanket as one young child knocks on the door of a palace hoping to take refuge from the snow. Chimes sound, the door is opened, and the king and his new queen come face to face with a precious little girl holding a small black pouch.

Although she is safe and warm inside the walls of this palace, she is unable to communicate with the adults. The king looks at her long and hard, and is overcome when he realizes that she is his long-lost daughter. But, the new queen refuses to believe that she is a princess and relays her message to the king by calling her names.

Sitting at the dinner table, the little girl is quiet and unresponsive. At times she would twirl and play with the rocks in her pouch. Not wanting to be understanding or realize that this young child had a special disability, the queen continued her rants and raves about her not being a real princess, and was determined to prove it to the king by trying to demean her rock collection, but the king counteracts her words. But, why not make her realize that she is being mean and unfair to this precious little girl?

Wanting to prove herself right, she decides to test the child. With the help of the royal butler she sets out to prove the little girl is a fake. Her special royal ruby is the bait. The mean queen places it under a pile of mattresses to see if the little girl could feel it, ala *The Princess and the Pea.* The ability to feel it under the mattresses is the true test of a real princess.

The queen piles the mattresses high, hoping the little princess won't feel a thing. What happens will definitely surprise the queen, but will it be enough to make her be kind to her stepdaughter?

The young princess is Autistic and has difficulty communicating with others. Just what will happen when the queen realizes the truth about the princess? Will she understand that she is special even though she has trouble communicating with others? Will she embrace her as a true member of her family?

Once again, author Jewel Kats and illustrator Richa Kinra bring a story to light that will have a great impact on everyone who reads it. The pictures are so lifelike and the colors are so vibrant that they tell the story in their own way as you see the faces of each character and their emotional responses to each other.

The Princess and the Ruby: An Autism Fairy Tale has many more chapters that can be written and more stories about other young children that can be told. Will the author bring our princess back and show the progress that she can make with the right help? Will she create more stories about children with Autism? This is just the beginning and what a powerful start.

A note about Autism

Helpguide.org includes an article titled *Autism Spectrum Disorders — A Parent's Guide to Symptoms and Diagnosis on the Autism Spectrum*. In part is says, "A spectrum disorder, meaning that there is a wide degree of variation in the way it affects people. Every child on the autism spectrum has unique abilities, symptoms, and challenges. Learning about the different autism spectrum disorders will help you better understand your own child, get a handle on what all the different autism terms mean, and make it easier to communicate with the doctors, teachers, and therapists helping your child."

Autism awareness is vital as is understanding that these children are highly intelligent, can learn, and will be able to communicate with others with the help of the right teachers, doctors, and support from their family. This book will enlighten readers, and I encourage sharing this book with schools, doctors, guidance counselors, young children and parents.

THE SECRETS THEY KEPT: THE TRUE STORY OF A MERCY KILLING THAT SHOCKED A TOWN AND SHAMED A FAMILY

Author: Suzanne Handler
Page count: 152
ISBN: 978-0-9885639-0-2
Formats: Paperback, ebook
Find the author: www.SuzanneHandler.com

REVIEW BY FRAN LEWIS

After a life-changing secret comes is revealed, Suzanne Handler struggles to make sense of her family history in this true story.

Painters create portraits in order to preserve the image of the person who is spotlighted within the frame. The colors on the pallet often depict the person's mood, demeanor, and personality. We also do that in our minds with those we, creating an image based on what we believe we know about people. When something comes along to drastically change our perception of that person, the mental portrait we've held dear for so long no longer works.

Sam Levin was a family man, tormented by something that would change his family's dynamic even after his death. Life often presents challenges and obstacles that we must face, but what happens when your daughter hands you an obstacle that could destroy a family's trust and love and create more than just one degree of separation between those that remain?

Secrets have a way of coming out when least expected. Imagine visiting your favorite aunt for a happy occasion and having your whole world shattered within seconds. One single revelation sends Suzanne Handler on a quest to find the truth, the hidden realities and the reasons why Sam Levin, her beloved grandfather, committed murder. The secret that's revealed will shatter her life in more ways than one.

She sets out to find out why her grandfather, a man whose life was devoted to his family, who was strong-minded, and who was admired by the members of his community, would take the life of his own child. Handler found it hard to believe when her aunt revealed that her grandfather once had a daughter named Sally who was diagnosed with dementia praecox—schizophrenia. She was even more shocked to learn that he took her life in order to spare her one spent within the walls of an insane asylum.

Suzanne's world crumbled. How could this wonderful man take a gun and shoot his own daughter? We learn more about the murder and the incident is graphically revealed. We hear the voice of Sam Levin and that of Sally pleading with him to end her life. It was her final request.

August 16, 1937, is a date Suzanne will never forget. She and the rest of the members of her family learn the startling truth behind the murder after receiving a packet of information from one of her cousins in California. They read the articles, see the documents related to the investigation, and hear Sally's voice loud and clear as they try and understand *The Secrets They Kept*, and the final fate of this family.

Author Suzanne Handler takes readers back to the beginning, and shares the day that Sally died. We learn another secret that will be challenged by others and make us wonder what the real truth is and what really happened that day. The vivid description of that day is compelling, heartbreaking, and yet in some respects unclear. What happened to Sally is quite apparent, but what happened to Sam leaves many unanswered questions in the reader's mind.

Two separate pacts were made as a result of Sally's death. One pact was between father and daughter, and a second is revealed later in the book. Sally, in her own way, realized she had mental health problems. Her actions were uncontrollable, violent, and she was a danger to herself and to others. Knowing that she would be confined to an institution for the mentally insane, she pleads with her father to take her life.

Was this murder or a mercy killing? You, the reader, will have to decide after you read the facts, hear her story, and understand more about Sam Levin and his family. Articles and documentation provided by the author are related to not only the incident, but also the charges filed against Sam.

Gossip flies in Cheyenne, the small town where the Levin family lived. News of Sally's death and Sam's role in it spread through the town, changing people's attitudes towards him, and tarnishing his name. This was on top of the shame brought on by the stigma of a family member with mental illness. Two prominent doctors decide Sam's fate and determine whether he was sane when he pulled the trigger.

Three months after Sally's death, an officer of the court would assess the facts and relate Sam's reasons for committing the crime and his failed attempt to take his own life to a judge. Sam said there was a pact made between him and his daughter that they would leave the earth together. So, when his attempt failed, why didn't Sam try again and finish what he started? Did he realize what he had done was wrong?

You will understand how and when she was diagnosed, his rationale, and much more. The author also includes the Mourner's Kaddish, which in the Jewish faith is said after the burial — and possibly every day for one year, it is also said on Yom Kippur, the last day of Passover, and on the anniversary of the person's death each year.

The author reflects on Sally's death and wonders whether anyone honored her by visiting her grave, saying prayers for her, or even having a headstone placed as a marker in front of her grave. The author includes the rituals of the Jewish Funeral, the grieving period, and explains Shiva. We learn that her headstone states her name, that she was their daughter, when she was born and when she died. Her first name, Sally, was misspelled, and no one had paid for the stone.

The author relates Sally's life story, why she was called Blackie, and the abuse she took at the hands of family members and friends. Sally was an average student but had few friends. The author also includes, for the reader, the definitions needed to understand Sally's illness.

We also learn that her own mother refused to speak about Sally. The information Suzanne learned was mainly obtained from her research, since every family member she questioned refused to tell her anything. One uncle went so far as to say that she should never speak of Sally again. The author includes information about family dynamics and when Sally and others noticed her mental decline as well as the family's second pact — silence. You will not believe the secrets they kept and why they all refused to discuss Sally. This poor young woman's family wanted to pretend that she'd never existed.

The author tells about her life and interaction with her grandfather as she debates the question of whether he was a mercy slayer or murderer. We also learn more about her grandmother, who was described as fearful, unstable, and showing little emotion. This makes us wonder if Sally's illness might be linked to her.

We then learn about Sam Levin's life growing. How he grew up, his religious affiliations, coming to America from Russia, dealing with the pogroms, and what lengths he went to in order to support his family. Learn why he chose to live in Omaha, Nebraska, how and why he became a homesteader, and about the Galveston Movement.

The author includes Levin's Naturalization Certificate, Patent Record, and Warranty Deed. She also goes into more detail about Sally Levin; her diagnosis and the history behind this illness, relating it back to colonial America and a prominent psychiatrist named Rush, who it is believed is the first to posit, "Mental illness is a disease of the mind, rather than a possession of demons."

The author exposes secrets, deception, lies, betrayals in her one-woman crusade to find answers about Sally's life and death. Jewish law, rituals, and the final verdict fill the pages of the chapter titled "The Good Death: You Decide!" The author discusses Jewish law related to euthanasia and assisted suicide, Sam's relationship with the Jewish community, and the effect of the death on the community are discussed. He was one man who struggled with his thoughts, conscience, motives, and love for a child and gave up his freedom, his own life, and bore shame upon himself in order to honor her final request.

Secrets — they can do more than just tear a family apart; they can divide it forever. Suzanne Handler is haunted by what she does not know, what she found out, and whether anything could have prevented the chain of events that caused one family to discount the existence of one of its members.

The research is extensive for this heartbreakingly vivid story. The voice of the author — her thoughts, feelings, and frustrations —comes through loud and clear. The final chapter will bring tears to your eyes, and the epilogue will allow you to remember Sally and those who have passed within your own family. In her memory I said Kaddish, and to those in her family, you need to remember her and say The El Male Rachamim when you visit her grave.

I dedicate this review to the memory of Sally and others whose lives matter and should not be forgotten.~Fran

MONDAYS WITH MARY

Author: Sam Oliver
Page count: 114
ISBN: 978-1-60414-563-2
Formats: Paperback, ebook
Find the author: www.PathIntoHealing.com

REVIEW BY FRAN LEWIS

Within your heart lay your innermost thoughts, fears, and desires. Life does not always present itself in the way we would like, and we have to learn how to deal with its many obstacles on our journey from beginning to end. In *Monday's with Mary*, Jim was a counselor working with many patients in a Hospice setting. He worked to provide them with the ability to analyze their thoughts to allow their emotions to come to the surface to help them evaluate their life experiences. This was not an easy task.

Jim often visits another dimension while asleep, which allows him to release his own tensions, and feel the weight of his body reduced to that of a feather so he can experience peace. Author Sam Oliver creates a sleeping world for Jim that is filled with gardens below him, and mountains, water, and lakes that are described with such amazing clarity that you feel you're there. It even seems like you can hear the splashing of the water, see the ripples as if someone dropped a pebble, and view the magnificent horizon.

Then a vision of a man took hold and he is no longer alone. Imagine being in the Garden of Gods and meeting the Angel of Promise. Why he was drawn to him will be revealed as the Angel explains he is concerned about the unrest in Jim's heart, and feels the need for him to communicate with him about it.

The angel explains that this garden helps us to connect to "all that ever has been, is, and will be." This secret garden will allow you to find the place your soul calls home. Within this garden and your heart, you will understand your inner thoughts, feelings, and dreams that can relate to your everyday life.

Jim needs to find and visit his creative side. To do this, he contacts his friend, Elizabeth, who runs a volunteer program. She introduces him to a man named Larry, and from there things change for Jim, as does his perspective on life and how to help others. Looking for the good in a person and showing how to expand and appreciate their lives is part of what Larry does.

Jim meets Mary when Larry takes a leave of absence and Elizabeth pairs them because she thinks that they would work well together. Jim realizes Mary is special. She has very little time left; yet she understands life and its true meaning. She teaches Jim about the importance of taking time for his emotions and himself. They discuss the Angel of Promise, and how this special he encourages them both to embrace life and their innermost thoughts. Jim learns that he needs to take time to really hear what others say, to look deep within his heart, breathe, and focus harder on the words of others in order to help them.

Mary explains that Jim needs to release control of his environment with words and let the language of his soul emerge into unconditional love; this will let his mind expand. As Jim recalls his feelings for his first grade teacher, Ms. Bee, he realizes that what he really learned and felt was the joy of learning that she imparted to him and her students. She did what all educators would do in a perfect world — instilled the love for learning and sharing knowledge in all her students' hearts.

When I write a review, the words seem to come to me as I place my hands on the keyboard and allow my thoughts to flow naturally without even thinking about the words that are being written. Someone once asked me how I could read a book and find the soul of it and understand the author's message. After experiencing Jim and Mary's story, I think I finally understand something that I never really thought about before. When you open your heart and "allow Eternity to breathe in through you, and your mind and heart expand; these moments are called Inspiration."

Jim finds that he is making a difference in the world because of his writing and that is why he is here. Sharing his feelings is like a bridge between Heaven and Earth. He now understands that writers are vehicles to explain the awareness given to us in thoughts and set them forth in written form.

All of this has prepared Jim to deal with the relationship with Mary, who is dying. He found his heart awaken into an eternal love as he discovered his true nature. Close your eyes and you, too, might hear the Angel Promise. Listen to your heart, silence your mind, and welcome the wisdom into your life. Within all of us is a choice-maker who allows us to choose what we want out of life. That choice-maker, Mary states through the author, is the Real You — your eternal nature.

As the story unfolds, Mary can no longer communicate, so Jim needs to listen closely to things other than her voice. He understands that he will always hear her voice, and she will always be with him. Can you feel her presence? Do you see her face? Do you see the Golden Light? When you open your heart, mind, and soul and find the place where unconditional love exists and your most sacred thoughts and desires are, Mary says, you will break free of conditions and you, too, will know where she is and exists.

Death is hard to deal with, and the living sometimes needs to understand their purpose in life and share it with others. The ending of the book is different from what you might expect, and only one person can teach the final lessons that Jim learns. You will have to read and interpret the end for yourself.

Author Sam Oliver gives the reader much to think about and a unique perspective on how we should deal with many different situations in life. He shows how a relationship, even a short one with someone who is dying, can enrich our lives forever. *Monday's With Mary* is a special book that will help anyone that wants to find his or her inner self and unconditional love. When you read it, you will understand where Mary is and what Jim has learned. When your creative imagination enters places you remember from your youth, you will allow yourself to open your heart and mind and take yourself on that journey with Jim and Mary, and allow yourself to be open to so many wonderful life-changing possibilities.

This book gets FIVE GOLDEN ANGELS NAMED MARY.

SUDC: Sudden Unexplained Death in Childhood

LEVI'S STORY

By Barbara Watkins

I imagine that many of you are not familiar with 'SUDC' — Sudden Unexplained Death in Childhood. In telling 'Levi's Story' — I hope to bring much needed attention to the subject. I want to personally thank Levi's family for kindly granting me permission to include the accounts of that tragic day in which SUDC claimed the life of their only son — forever changing their lives. As well, I want to thank, Laura Crandall, MA — Program Director / Co-Founder & SUDC Parent, for graciously giving me permission to include educational and valuable information obtained from the SUDC Program web site, www.sudc.org

The following is a written account from, http://www.levisadventuretrail.com of the moments leading up to the tragic loss of their precious little angel, Levi, as told by his Mother, Ellie Collom:

"Levi woke up on Saturday, March 17th 2012 with a slight fever. He snuggled up with his sister on the couch that morning while they watched cartoons. That is a memory that I cherish. He told me he wasn't feeling well and he was cold. I took his temperature and it was around 100. I gave Levi some Motrin and he began to feel better. Our family left the house and went to Cape for lunch and did a little shopping. We went to a local restaurant and Levi played in the children's area and had the biggest smile on his face. We even stayed extra long because he was having so much fun. We headed home after that and Levi and Glenn (his daddy) played in the backyard.

Victoria and I left to go to Sikeston because I had a contract that needed to sign for a house that I sold (one that I will never be able to go into again). I remember telling Levi bye, and that I loved him. He still had the biggest smile on his face. He was in our backyard playing on his John Deere 4 wheeler and his swing set. My only regret is that I didn't go give him a hug and a kiss.

Glenn said that not long after we left the house they came inside. Levi fell asleep on the couch and Glenn carried him into his bedroom so he could nap comfortably. Glenn said that after about an hour or so he went in to check on Levi. Levi woke up and told his daddy he was still sleepy and wasn't ready to get up yet. This was a common thing, so Glenn though nothing about it.

Glenn went downstairs and about 10 minutes later he heard a noise. He went back upstairs to check on Levi and that is when he found him face first in his toddler bed. Glenn rolled him over and saw that Levi was not breathing and had no pulse. He started CPR and called 911. The sheriff's dept. and EMT's were at the house quickly.

Levi was taken to an area hospital ER where they worked on him for several hours. They said they got his heart to beat again but that he kept having cardiac arrest. A children's hospital from St. Louis brought their nurses down to take Levi to St. Louis. When he got to St Louis they were worked on him for nearly 8 hours and they could not bring him back to us.

Levi died on the morning of March 18th, 2012.

In our hearts we know that Levi was gone when Glenn found him, but because of advancement in medical procedures they were able to get his heart beating by medicine only and after some time his body was rejecting all of those advanced procedures.

We were all able to hold Levi while he died. I was holding him, his daddy was holding his head and his Mimi was holding his feet, while grandma Bobbie was touching him. We were all there when his body stopped. When this happened I felt like I was in a fog.

There were two things that were very difficult after that. One, I had to tell Victoria that her brother didn't make it and see her face and two, we had to leave him in St. Louis and drive home without him. That was the emptiest feeling a parent can ever experience.

One thing that makes no sense is how a healthy child that is over SIDS age (12 months) can go to sleep and not wake up. The fog of confusions still follows me to this day. We have found a support group where there are many other families that have suffered the exact tragic event that we have. Finding this group was a relief but has also been heart breaking. There are families introduced from around the world that have lost their toddler aged children just like Levi. I have never heard of this; how can this happen to so many other people?"

Levi Stephen Collom was a happy, healthy 3-1/2 year old boy that died unexpectedly and with no answers. He was the precious son of Glenn Collom and Ellie Woods Collom — the baby brother of Victoria Collom – the grandson to Steve and Viney Mosley, Bobbie Collom and the late Charles Collom and Steve Woods, and great-grandson of Maxine Woods and the late James Woods.

This family and every family affected by 'SUDC' struggles every minute of every second of the day to understand why — they deserve our attention and they deserve answers.

As stated on the sudc.org web site – sudden unexplained death in childhood is rare, with a reported incidence in the United States of 1.4 deaths per 100,000 children, compared to 54 deaths per 100,000 live births for SIDS in 2009. It is not surprisingly therefore, that there is very little known in the medical literature about SUDC.

Medical research in this area has never been more important than it is right now. Under the 'Advocacy' link on the www.sudc.org web site, you can show your support by encouraging your congressmen to cosponsor crucial legislation, Bill S.314/H.R.669 that will further improve investigations into children that die unexpectedly under the age of 4, as well as still-birth deaths.

The Collom family is living a day-to-day nightmare that only we can imagine happening in our most haunting dream. However, with the grace of God, love of family, friends and the determination to pay honor to their little angel, Levi — the concept of Levi's Adventure Trail was born. It will be an interactive outdoor exhibit at the Discovery Playhouse Children's Museum in Cape Girardeau, Mo. As a family they often enjoyed weekends on Current River in nearby, Van Buren, Mo. — one of Levi's favorite places to go. The exhibit will have a camping area for children that might not otherwise be able to enjoy such an experience — leaping logs and curious caves included. For more information about this extraordinary exhibit visit, the Facebook page. And, donations are always welcome. And thus out of this unspeakable tragedy, Levi's spirit continues to inspire everyone that knew him, and to capture the love of those new to his story.

On the front of the SUDC web site you will be welcomed with this message,

"We are dedicated to increasing awareness of sudden unexpected deaths in childhood, funding crucial research into the causes and prevention of SUDC, and advocating for the needs of families affected by these tragedies. We are the only organization worldwide devoted solely to the needs of families and professionals touched by unexplained death in childhood."

I urge you to visit their site to learn more about SUDC, www.sudc.org

Levi's Wings of Gold

God has called you home my little one,
to where it all began.
In Heaven you are an angel with wings of gold.
Here on earth, you were our little man.
And while God granted us but just a few short years with your soul,
we are promised to be united forever when it's our time to go.
I say the same prayer every night, when I lay my head down and close my eyes.
I pray God will send you back to me, if not only in a dream.
Then the miracle happens;
I see your smiling face; feel your tender soft skin against mine.
We run and play along the riverbed and though it is but just a dream, it is yet another sweet visit I will treasure until we meet again.
So spread your wings of gold sweet angel as you dance to a lullaby in the night.
Mommy and Daddy will look to the heavens holding onto your memory tight with the words flowing from our lips 'we love you forever' as we blow you a kiss goodnight.

Barbara Watkins resides in Missouri with her husband and loyal boxweiler, Hooch. In her writings, she loves to evoke a false sense of security and expectations, as she leads her reader into a world of the unknown. Her articles on various subjects, short stories, and poetry, have appeared in 2008 *New York Skyline Review,* and several on-line publications. *Cold Coffee Magazine* accepted her article, "A Testament To Poets," for their second issue released in print and is available online at *Cold Coffee Magazine.*

In 2010, Watkins collaborated with New Zealand director, Dimi Nakov, on a screenplay for a short movie titled "BlindSide." Her name appears at the film's end credits for voice-over monologue. "BlindSide" was accepted into the Cannes short film corner as part of the 65th Festival de Cannes as well as the 7th Cyprus International Film Festival 2012, and many more prestigious film festivals.

Many of her short stories and novella, *Thorns of an Innocent Soul,* have been optioned to New Zealand film production company, Zodiac Entertainment, for screenplay adaptation to film.

Previous Publications: *Mortal Abomination — Awaken Spirit — Hollowing Screams — Six-Pack of Blood* (co-author, Betty Dravis) *Six-Pack of Fear* (co-author, Betty Dravis). Anthologies include, *Hope Whispers* (compiled by Lynn C. Johnston) *Live Life: The Daydreamer's Journal* (compiled by Sir Ricky McGentleman) *Satan's Holiday*, an anthology of scary stories (compiled by Yvonne Mason) and *Writing Tips From Authors* (compiled by Patti Roberts.)

Visit her website: www.barbarawatkins.net

POP STARS ARE HUMAN, TOO

By Marti Smiley Childs and Jeff March

Although we tend to think of pop stars as leading glamorous lives, surrounded by luxury, that's only an elusive dream for the majority of working musicians. Writing and recording music requires great discipline. And going on the road on concert tours is grueling, tiring work. Looking fresh and vibrant on stage after hours of travel, commitment to appear on stage despite headaches, muscle aches, the flu or other ailments, being separated from family members — all of those hardships take their toll.

On top of that, many musicians find that they are unable to sustain a living from the entertainment business. Consequently, many musicians have made the practical but painful choice to seek their livelihoods from other occupations. For our first book *Echoes of the Sixties* (Billboard Books 1999, re-released by EditPros LLC in 2011 as an e-book) and for our more recent books *Where Have All the Pop Stars Gone? — Volumes 1* and *2* (EditPros LLC 2011, 2012*)*, we interviewed 90 pop music performers whose recordings hit the national charts during the 1960s.

Many of the pop stars with whom we spoke chose to leave the business after confronting personal problems, such as substance abuse and drug dependency, as well as to respond to the needs of family members who have developmental disabilities or other impairments. Two members of the Association, whose impeccable harmonies and brilliant musical arrangements distinguish one of the most talented groups of the 1960s, spoke candidly to us about their struggles in *Where Have All the Pop Stars Gone? - Volume 1.*

Overcoming chemical dependency

After a highly successful music career with numerous hits to his performing and composing credit (including writing the mammoth hit *Cherish*), and several years as a writer and producer of commercials, ads and movie trailers, Terry Kirkman discovered a new sense of fulfillment as a chemical dependency counselor, consultant and teacher. Overcoming his own struggles with chemical dependency in 1984 and helping to run a recovery program in Hollywood Community Hospital opened a new pathway to his personal development and self-contentment.

"I am a recovering alcoholic. I was a screaming cocaine addict. And I got sober on October 21, 1984, six weeks after leaving the Association, and I've remained so ever since."

Through his own recovery activities, Terry was invited to work in a recovery program at Hollywood Community Hospital. The experience proved to be fulfilling and Terry decided to return to school to pursue a career in chemical dependency counseling. After working for many public and private facilities, Terry opened a small private practice in Los Angeles, counseling chemically dependent people and their families. In 2000, he became the clinical director of the Musicians' Assistance Program (MAP) in Hollywood. MAP was a nonprofit, independent organization founded in 1995 by a recovering addict, professional jazz sax player Buddy Arnold. Its purpose was to assist people in the music business overcome problems with substance abuse. Terry handled the assessment; referral and funding of treatment for people in the music business throughout the country in need of professional help. MAPS became part of MusicCares, a division of the Grammy Foundation.

"There's no comparison to anything else I've done in my life. It was one of the best jobs I could ever imagine having in the recovery profession," he says. "Someone would call up all helpless and hopeless and broke, and if they met our minimal requirements, I could have them in a treatment facility within minutes. Totally free, if needed. I'd go home with a great feeling of gratitude every night."

In addition, Terry has served as a consultant for sober-living facilities, including a facility that houses members of the homeless population with the purpose of re-entering them into functional, independent living. "By and large, in an urban setting, 60 to 70 percent of anybody who walks into a regular general therapist's office is either chemically dependent or greatly impacted by someone who is chemically dependent. Eighty-five percent of inmates in the California penal system are there because of drug- and alcohol-related crimes. It's just like fighting a war," he said.

For the love of an autistic child

Most people would agree that 20 years at any career, let alone sticking with the same band, is unusual and admirable. And if you've been on the road for any period of time, you'll know that burnout is a common reason for calling it quits. However, it was for the love of family that drummer Ted Bluechel made the painstaking decision to leave the Association in 1984 – the year his wife, Carol, gave birth to son Michael. Born three months premature, Michael experienced some health problems that resulted in autism.

"I wanted to stay on, doing what I could do as time would allow, but we have a motto in the group — you're either in the group or you're out of the group. So I really had no choice but to cut the cord and step back," says Bluechel. When he left the group, Ted Bluechel's resume read "singer and drummer in the Association," which he had done since he was 21 years old.

He looked for jobs that would cause him the least amount of stress, because he'd endured enough for a lifetime being on the road for so many years. "Stress is a big factor that has had its way with me, but as I'm getting older, I really look to enjoy what's left of the span here on Earth. I just go on looking after my own household."

Music fever crept back into Ted's life in about 1994, when he began performing with a trio called Sweet and Dandy. "That was a lot of fun for a while, but then one of the guys went his own way, and I needed to replace him. I'd done that so many times during the '70s with the Association. I got tired of repairing the group's sound and putting it back together again every two or three months, so I just went solo. It was a lot less trouble, and I don't have to argue with anybody."

In 1999 Ted began his solo career (billed as Ted Bluechel) in clubs in the Ventura, Camarillo, Thousand Oaks and Santa Barbara areas. He says his favorite Association songs are "Never My Love" and "Windy," which he performs with a mix of other popular '60s tunes, some Jimmy

Buffet tunes, a taste of Jamaican and Caribbean West Indies music, and some of his own original material.

"I'm choosing to stay in the slow lane. Anything you choose in the fast lane means going on the road, and I've had it with the road. I'm just sort of enjoying doing what I'm doing and sharing my life with Carol and Michael."

Marti Smiley Childs and Jeff March are partners in EditPros LLC, writing, editing, and publishing firm they established in 1993. They are coauthors of the three pop stars books mention in the article: *Where Have All the Pop Stars Gone? – Volumes 1 and 2* and *Echoes of the Sixties,* as well as being publishers of *Within My Grasp: A Double Amputee's True Story* (written with Mike Penketh and published in spring 2013), and *Reckoning at Sea: Eye to Eye With a Gray Whale* (written with Max J. Young and published in summer 2013). All of the books are available as both paperbacks and ebooks.

WHAT'S HAPPENING TO US?

Mark Rubinstein

Let me begin by saying I have a desktop, a laptop, a tablet, an e-reader and a smartphone. I use them all and think they're great technologic advances. In certain obvious ways, they're a boon. So I'm not some version of Grandpa Cranky-Pants complaining about the role of technology in our lives.

But something strange is definitely happening.

I read an article saying the average person checks his or her smart phone 150 times per day! This seemed unbelievable, so I read another article. It said 58 percent of smartphone users check their phones at least every hour, and a large number check them while in bed or in the bathroom. When at a meal with someone, 30 percent of people admit to checking their phones. When driving, 24 percent acknowledge checking their phones (ibid) behind the wheel.

Mental health professionals debate whether Internet addiction should be a diagnosable disorder, and experts have discussed various reasons for people's obsession with cell phones.

Seventy-three percent of people (according to the same study) admitted they would feel "panicked" if they lost their devices.

Is there really something called Nomophobia — intense fear of being *disconnected* because one's cell phone is not available? (*Nomophobia* is derived from "*No Mo*bile Phone Phobia").

Is there such a thing as "digital addiction"? Do you know a camp exists in California, called Camp Grounded, where adults go for *digital detoxification*?

On a more personal level, I've been in restaurants and have seen couples at nearby tables where the man and woman stare at and are busily thumbing/scrolling/ or tapping their smart phones. They barely talk with each other. I've seen two couples at a restaurant table, each person has a cell phone on the table and there is frequent checking. It's not even considered rude when in the middle of an exchange, one person reaches for a cell phone after it's dinged or beeped. I've been in restaurants where someone at my own table received a text and began texting back—and literally absented herself from the company at hand. It was really annoying.

On a Metro North train last week, ready to exit at my stop, I looked about the car. Every person—young, old, men, women, teens—was deeply engrossed in using a smartphone or tablet. Each was scrolling, thumbing, reading, or talking on a device. No one was talking to anyone present. It was weird.

Okay, so we're changing as a society. There's now instant interconnectedness, a readily accessible digital stream of information and ease of communication with other people, even if they live continents away.

But let's look a little closer at the price we pay.

What if:

The conversation is banal and involves simply saying you're going to a coffee shop, and you're *speeding* obliviously through a supermarket parking lot.

What once was considered rude (breaking away from a face-to-face conversation to talk to someone else or check a text message) has now become the norm.

People frequently check for e-mails, texts, news or weather updates when there's no real reason to do so.

These phone checking habits blunt interaction with those actually present.

Some mental health professionals find commonalities between these behaviors and substance abuse. Some see them as part of a "compulsive-impulsive spectrum disorder" (along with compulsive gambling, shopping, or excessive credit card use).

A recent article in the *Journal of Behavioral Addictions* showed young adults send out an average of 3,200 text messages per month.

Fifty-four percent of people check their phones while lying in bed (same study as cited above).

Many people can't get through a meal without a quick Facebook or e-mail check.

Most people acknowledge their phone checking/scrolling/texting behavior is severely heightened when sitting alone in a public place, like a restaurant. It makes me wonder *what happened to people enjoying the occasional pleasure of their own company.*

We know the role cell phones play in traffic accidents.

Some Asian countries have established rehab centers for video gaming among young people.

As a psychiatrist, I wonder if technology use is turning us into a device-obsessed, remotely-accessed, digitally enhanced people where *true* relatedness is dampened and taking a back seat to digital connections. Communication with each other has never been easier, but are we really relating?

The jury may still be out. But it's a conversation worth having.

Mark Rubinstein has coauthored five medical self-help books: *The First Encounter: The Beginnings in Psychotherapy*, *The Complete Book of Cosmetic Facial Surgery*, *New Choices: the Latest Options in Treating Breast Cancer*, *Heartplan: A Complete Program for Total Fitness of Heart & Mind*, and *The Growing Years: A Guide to Your Child's Emotional Development from Birth to Adolescence*, and wrote the novels *Mad Dog House*, named a Finalist for the 2012 ForeWord Reviews Book of the Year Award (Thriller & Suspense), and *Love Gone Mad*. www.MarkRubinstein-Author.com

BRAND NEW DAY

Janet Yarkowsky isn't a real person, nor is she based on anyone I know. Her story came to me in dreams over a series of nights—strange for someone who never remembers her dreams. I felt compelled to sort through the words and images given to me and I hope I have written a true and cohesive version of the story. This story really touched my heart. I hope it will also touch yours. ~ Dellani

CHAPTER 1

Lubbock, Texas — May 2000

Janet May Yarkowsky lay in bed shivering from withdrawal. Whatever Tex had given her was making her crazy. She had a vague memory of events the night before. The only thing outstanding in her mind was that she'd stood there placidly as he'd threatened to kill her eldest son.

How could I do that? How could I let him threaten Danny? What if next time he doesn't just wave the gun around? What if, somehow, he finds out the truth? That Danny isn't his. What then?

Another fit of shakes gripped her body as she huddled under the tangled covers. She had to fix this. Had to stop Tex before his hatred and drug augmented paranoia drove him to kill.

She knew Danny wouldn't leave her like this, not forever. He left her last night because she'd been crazy too. Standing, frozen, on the porch, staring like a zombie while Tex threatened her boys with a sawed off.

Danny did the only thing he could. He took Ricky away. He called his aunt and uncle and they picked the boys up, carrying them to safety.

How did I let it get like this? She asked the wall, but it had no answer. *I loved him once, didn't I? Danny, what would you do if you knew Tex wasn't your daddy? Would you kill him? Beat the hell out of him like he richly deserves?*

She couldn't tell him and prayed he wouldn't find out on his own. Another man had her first. A man she loved more than her own life. But it wasn't meant to be.

"If only..." she whispered to the four walls. "If only..."

Scottsbluff, Nebraska — August 1975

"Janet May, get your lazy butt outta that bed. NOW!"

Sookie, her baby sister, turned on the lights and threw back the covers. Janet had ducked under to get away from the blazing lights. Sookie yanked her hair trying to get the blankets off.

"Mama said get up outta that bed now!" Sookie did everything Mama said. Frequently, that was torturing Janet. "Get up now!"

"Sookie Ann, you leave me be! I still got five minutes."

"Mama said..."

"Mama didn't say to scream like a banshee and be a unholy terror."

"First day of school!" Sookie yelled. "It's the *first day*!"

"I know that!" Janet bellowed, sitting up in bed. "I'm awake, blast it. Leave me be."

She threw her pillow for emphasis, clipping Sookie on the rear end. Her little sister howled like she was being killed.

"Mama!" Sookie wailed.

Their mother stormed in, on Sookie's side—as usual.

"I hit her with a *pillow*," Janet said before her mother yelled. "She turned on the light, yanked my hair and nearly snatched me bald. Jerked back the covers like I can't get up on my own." Her alarm clock went off. "See? I was gonna give myself five whole minutes. I swear, Mama, y'all treat me like like a baby!"

Janet stormed out of the room and headed to the bathroom for a shower. It was hot and muggy. She wanted to be fresh her first day. She wasn't in three minutes, hadn't even soaped her hair, when Sookie banged on the door, yelling.

"Mama says — get out!"

"I will when I'm done!"

"Mama said *now*!"

"Mama can come her own self and tell me. Go away, Sookie."

"Janet May!"

"Sookie Ann, swear to God!" She cut off the water.

Dripping and furious, she flung open the door. Sookie stood there looking smug, arms crossed over her flat, ten year old chest.

Janet shoved past her, walking toward the kitchen. "Did you send that little brat to get me?" she demanded of her mother.

"You got to catch the bus..."

"Mama, I know how to get ready. I'm fifteen."

"First day of high school, I want to see you off."

"I'm not a baby like Sookie! I been taking care of both of us forever!"

"There's no need to talk to me like that."

"There is a need! There's been a need since daddy left. But I was too young to know. It's not my fault he's gone."

Her mother stiffened. "You saying it's mine?"

"You're the one he argued with, not me. Daddy *loved* me."

"He loved you so much he left?"

"He told me — before he left. He told me — 'Girls belong with their mamas' or he'd take me. He told me he loved me and he was sorry, but he had to get away."

"So, then he just left you, huh? All alone with your mean old mama?" The tone of her voice stung more than her words.

Janet wanted to cry, but with Sookie and Mama both glaring at her, she wouldn't let the tears come. She dressed in a fury. Angry, hurt tears burned in her eyes. She didn't say goodbye, just grabbed her lunch she'd made the night before, and left. She slammed the door behind her, starling some birds in the trees next door.

Sookie wasn't at the bus stop. She hadn't expected her to be. Mama didn't want her baby girl on the bus with all the big kids, afraid she'd get hurt. It was okay that Janet had ridden the bus since kindergarten, big kids or not. The bus wasn't good enough for Miss Sookie. It was just as well. Janet didn't want people to know they were related.

Janet's friends were waiting for her, all dressed in their new clothing. Janet had saved her money from her job at the A&W Drive-In to buy her things. She looked just as fresh and nice as they did.

Her pink t-shirt had big, fuchsia rhinestone lips on the front. Her hot pants were denim. Her long, tanned legs made the other girls jealous, as did her full lips and black, curly hair.

They didn't know the *Secret* Janet carried inside her. If they did, she wondered how they'd act. She told everyone there was Indian blood way back, but that wasn't it. Her daddy was half Black, but didn't look it. He'd passed for years as a white man. Wasn't until Janet was born, a nice café au lait, with kinky curls, that her mama suspected.

That was how it started. Her Southern born mama couldn't forgive him for being Black. When Janet was four, he left them. They moved from Texas to Nebraska. Mama hooked up with some guy and Sookie was born about a year later.

Mama had kin in Nebraska, which was why they'd moved there. Kin that didn't know she'd married a Black man. She could hide her shame away, forget about him. Only every day, Janet was a reminder.

The bus pulled up and stopped. There was the usual tussle to see who got on first. Today, as always, the big boys won. They hopped on and took seats at the back. The girls let the little kids go on before them. Mr. Prost, the driver, told them thank you.

"I believe you girls have all grown at least three inches apiece," he said after greeting them each by name. "High school now. My, my."

Mr. Prost had been their bus driver as long as Janet could remember. He was a nice, grandfatherly type. Janet loved Mr. Prost and wished he was her granddaddy. Mama's father was a mean old cuss who smoked and drank too much. She'd never met her father's father. He was the *black sheep* and kept well hidden.

Bunny, her friend since second grade, bounced in the seat beside her. "I can't wait to get to high school! Betty says the boys are real cute!"

Betty was Bunny's older sister. Janet suspected she was boy crazy and had told Bunny so often enough.

"Not the ones we know," she said, cutting her eyes at the back of the bus.

"Those are sophomore boys!" Bunny rolled her eyes. "I mean juniors and seniors."

"What are those older boys gonna want with us?" Janet asked. "We're little kids compared to them."

"I know! They're men!" Bunny said with a dreamy sigh.

Janet made a disgusted noise. Come to think, Bunny was as boy crazy as her sister. The difference was, Bunny didn't sleep around like Betty did... Yet. She was a little afraid her friend was going to follow in her sister's footsteps.

"Junior high is behind us now," Bunny continued. "We're not around boys anymore. We're gonna be seeing real men every day."

"They're no more men than that bunch back there," Janet said.

"They aren't men until they're eighteen," Ramona said. "That's what my father says."

"Betty says they're real men once they make it with a girl," Bunny said with a toss of her head.

"Well, she's the expert," Ramona said dryly.

"What's that supposed to mean?" Bunny demanded.

"Nothing —" Ramona tossed her straight, black hair over her shoulder. "Oh, nothing —"

"Ramona Hernandez, you tell me!" Bunny growled. "What are you saying about my sister?"

"What *I* heard," Ramona said, ignoring her. "What *I* heard was that she's been through most of the male population. What *I* heard, is lots of the guys are men now because of Betty."

"Who told you a lie like that?" Bunny screeched.

Ramona flounced off the bus, ignoring Bunny's protestations. Janet knew Ramona's source was her older brother, Diego, who had more experience than just about any guy around. He never talked about it, but the girls did. Many of them had fallen for the dark haired, sloe eyed Mexican man. Janet could see the appeal, he was gorgeous. He'd only ever treated her like a sister, so she figured she didn't stand a chance. She could admire how good looking he was from a distance.

Diego had dated Betty until he found out how many guys she'd slept with. He didn't want to be one guy among the many. When he was with a girl, he was exclusive. He expected them to be the same.

Diego and his buddies were waiting for them at the bus loop. He drove a car and offered Ramona a ride, but she didn't want to crowd in the car with his loud, obnoxious friends. Diego wanted it clear to every man at the school that Ramona was his baby sister. He'd taken Bunny and Janet under his protective wing as well, since they had no older brothers. He put his arms possessively around the girls as they walked in the school surrounded by his huge, male friends.

All the guys were under strict rules, they couldn't touch the girls. Flirting was okay, hitting on was acceptable to an extent, but no touching. They touched, they got the hell beaten out of them. Diego had a reputation of being the toughest guy in school. He wasn't all that huge, there were guys plenty bigger who were terrified of him. But he was a swimmer, a boxer and a wrestler. He'd worked hard all his life and had muscles most guys were jealous of and girls drooled over.

Janet had heard some older women commenting about him once and one lady said he was an *Adonis*. Janet didn't know the word, but she went home and looked it up. She had to agree with the description. He was very handsome, almost godlike, with his dusky Latin looks.

Older girls watched as Diego and his buddies walked Ramona and the others to the auditorium for the opening assembly. Here, all their names would be read off by the assistant principal and they'd go to their first class. In that home room, they would get their class schedules.

"You gotta sit in the sophomore section," Diego told them, pointing to the right of center. "We sit in the senior section." He and his friends whooped, doing complicated handshakes.

The girls found seats together and sat down. Janet watched as Diego and his buddies walked to the front row of the center section and made the others there move so they could sit down. That would be their spot the rest of the year. No one would take it now that he'd claimed it.

"No guy is gonna want to ask me out," Ramona whined. "Why does he have to be like that? I've got the right to date who I want."

"I think it's sweet," Bunny said, gazing at Diego. "And he's so dreamy—"

"Stop that!" Ramona socked her. "He's my brother! You just keep those *Betty* thoughts to yourself."

"What's that supposed to mean?"

"She means don't be thinking you're going to seduce Diego," Janet said with a toss of her head. "Because he won't look at you twice. You're like his little sister."

She voiced what she was thinking about herself. She hadn't realized until today how fond she was of Ramona's older brother. She was off limits, his baby sister's best friend. She didn't have a chance.

The principal walked on the stage to polite applause. He gave his usual first day speech. Mr. Harper was a pretty cool guy. He was nice and he was fair. Most of the students got along well with him, unless they got on his bad side.

Mr. Patrick, the assistant principal, was the opposite. He was mean and rude, especially to the Mexican and Indian kids. He was also kind of dumb. He always mispronounced a bunch of student names when he read them off. He made mistakes with class assignments too, so the counselors would be busy for the next week fixing his errors.

Ramona's name was read as "Ramon A. Hernandez." She'd been assigned boy's PE as her first class. Mortified, she went to the office to wait her turn to get that changed to girl's PE.

Bunny Mason was called Benny and sent to health class. Finally, it was Janet's turn.

"Janet Yarsky," he said, butchering her last name.

At least he hadn't sent her somewhere embarrassing. She had to admit that Yarkowsky wasn't the easiest name and he hadn't done too badly. She followed her teacher to English class. That was her favorite subject. In fact, she hoped one day to be an English teacher.

The young male teacher, leading the group, looked like he'd be fun. He was dressed in the weirdest combination of clothing she'd ever seen. His pants were wide stripes of mustard yellow and maroon. His pullover sweater was an ugly green that reminded Janet of pond scum. The shirt was pale blue and his tie was several shades of brown. His chestnut hair was in kind of a shaggy Beetles cut and his blue eyes sparkled with happy enthusiasm. They got to the classroom and found seats. Fortunately, some of her friends were in the class.

"Hi, I'm Mr. Whitmore and this is Tenth Grade English. In here, we'll study literature and writing. I'm the debate coach, so we'll be giving that a try too. Maybe some of you will find out you like to argue."

"I love to argue," one big guy up front said with a grin. He waved his fists around.

Mr. Whitmore laughed. "Not that kind of arguing. Organized debate is more civilized."

The big guy snorted, shrugging.

"It's easy to cut a man down with your fists," Mr. Whitmore said quietly. "It's a lot harder to take him down with your words. In here, you'll learn to verbally spar."

The rest of the morning went pretty well. Janet had a couple of classes with Ramona and Bunny, then it was lunch time. In the cafeteria, the students had unofficial areas they sat in. The geeks and nerds sat in the corner talking about chess club and speaking in Latin. The stoners took their food to the parking lot where they ate and got smoked up before going back to class. Other groups were scattered around the cafeteria, all of them occupying most of the tables.

The girls stood there with their trays wondering where to sit. A piercing whistle got their attention. Diego waved to them, standing on a bench. Blushing, they walked over to the table. His big friends made room and the girls sat down. There were other girls there, girlfriends and wanna be's. Some frowned at Ramona, Janet and Bunny.

"What makes you think you can sit with us?" One girl in a tight white sweater said.

Diego had his arm around her shoulders, nibbling at her ear until she spoke. His arm left her shoulders and he shoved her away.

"Since it's my baby sister and her friends, *chica*. You be polite to my sister."

"Well, sor-ry," the girl said in a snotty tone. "I'm supposed to know?"

"They look just alike," Diego's best friend, Raul, said. "Pay some attention, *bruja*."

The girl raised her hand to hit him, but Diego grabbed her wrist.

"I don't think so. Take your stuff. Go," he said, nodding toward a different table. "Any you others got a problem with my girls sitting here?"

The other women smile pleasantly. "No problem, Diego," one girl said with a grin. "I've been wanting to meet you, Ramona," she said sweetly. "D. talks about you all the time. I'm Trina." She held out her hand.

They shook hands and Ramona introduced the others. Once Trina had introduced herself, the others followed. She seemed to be the female leader. She wasn't with Diego, she sat next to Raul. His arm hung around her shoulders, fingers teasingly close to her breast. Based on the hickies on their necks, they weren't just friends.

"What classes do you have after lunch?" Trina asked.

"Math," Bunny said, wrinkling her nose.

"Biology," Ramona added.

"I'm in Drama class," Janet said with a grin. "I can't wait. The Drama coach came to the junior high last year and taught a class. It was so much fun."

"I'm in there too," Trina said. "Mom Frost is awesome, isn't she?"

"Mom?"

Trina giggled, waving it away. "Tell you later. It's a long story just us Drama kids know. I'll take you over and introduce you. I've got rehearsal for the one acts at the speech meet next month. I'm a student director."

"Is it too late to try out?"

"Oh, we decided the cast at the end of last year. The season starts so soon, it's hard to take new people. But, there's all kinds of other things you can do for speech meets. Mom will talk about that today."

It was almost time for the bell, so they gathered their trays. The other girls befriended Ramona and Bunny, taking the younger girls to class. Diego watched as Janet and Trina walked off together. Raul punched him to get his attention.

"We'll be late for class, moron. Come on."

"Yeah. Coming."

"What's with you? All through lunch, you hardly said a word and you sent off what's-her-tits. You've been trying to get in that girl's panties forever."

"She insulted my sister. That disrespects me." He picked up his books, shoving past his friend.

"I never seen such a weird face on you, man," Raul said. "You're looking after my woman funny."

"No. Shit, no! I swear, man, not Trina."

Raul glanced over his shoulder. Trina was introducing Janet to people outside the Drama room across the commons.

"That Janet girl?" He laughed, punching his friend. "Man, she's not your style. Besides, she's a baby."

"She's no baby," Diego said with a muted sigh. "But she's sure a babe. How you mean she's not my style?"

"'Cause that girl will never let you in, bro."

Diego sighed again, this time more heavily. He swallowed hard, nodding as he took the stairs two at a time, heading to senior English. He sat in class, distracted by thoughts of Janet, his mind wandering, his chin rested on this hands.

"Are we boring you, Mr. Hernandez?" Mr. Franks, the English teacher said.

Diego blinked, sitting up straighter. "Uh, no sir."

"Perhaps you can tell me what we've been discussing."

"Yeah, sure." He thought a moment. "You're discussing the syllabus and you just mentioned *Julius Caesar*."

The class laughed. That was exactly what they'd been talking about—five minutes ago. Mr. Franks smirked.

"You'll stop with me after class, Mr. Hernandez."

"Yes, sir," he mumbled, slumping in his chair once more.

After class, Mr. Franks took him aside. He was a man in his late forties. Not unkind, but very strict. "Want to tell me what's on your mind? You're usually more focused. This is one of your best subjects."

"Nothing. It's not a big thing. . . ."

"Diego, I've known you forever. You've been my student for two years. I know when you're distracted by something."

Diego shrugged. He wouldn't meet Mr. Franks' eyes.

"What's her name?" Mr. Franks asked pointedly. He waited expectantly for Diego to answer.

"That obvious, huh? What an actor I am." He chuckled, shaking his head. "I'm gonna be late to class."

"I'll write you a note. Who?"

"She's new, you wouldn't know her. She's a friend of my sister's."

"Got it bad for her, huh? She tell you no?"

Diego laughed loudly. "I haven't asked her anything. She's my sister's best friend. I've known her since she was seven."

"And you're finding it hard to think of her as a sister anymore."

"Yeah. I'm sorry about daydreaming."

"Show her to me some time. I'll tell you if you deserve detention for it." The older man laughed, nudging him. He wrote a note for Diego and sent him to class.

Daydreaming about Janet in English class could have gotten Diego in trouble, but fortunately his teacher was cool about it. Somehow, he manges to finish out the day. When he walks into his last class, he doesn't realize he's in for a pleasant surprise.

CHAPTER 2

Diego's final class of the day was chorus. He'd been singing since he was a child. He sang in the church choir and he and his buddies were putting together a band with him at the head. He took his usual seat in the tenor section, dropping his books under the chair.

The door opened and a group of girls entered. A bubbling laugh rose above the others, filling the room with a joyful sound. Diego recognized that laugh. Janet had just walked in the room with his sister and Bunny.

Giggling and talking, they went to the soprano section and sat down. None of them noticed him until Trina walked in and waved at him and the girls. Ramona waved at her brother. He smirked, saluting.

"Nice you noticed me, *mi hermana*."

"I didn't know you'd be in here," she complained.

He chuckled, nodding. "Yeah, that's a good excuse. Don't embarrass me."

Ramona stuck her tongue out at him. Trina giggled and sat in the alto section with some of her friends. The bell rang and the teacher came out of his office. He looked at the students on risers and smiled.

"Welcome, everyone. I'm Mr. Carter, chorus teacher. Shall we begin?" He gestured to one of the girls who took her place at the piano.

The girl played a chord and each section took their pitch. They began their vocal warm-up, going higher and higher until it was out of the range of most of the chorus. Only Ramona, Janet and Bunny could hit the notes. Mr. Carter nodded to the pianist, encouraging her to go on. Moments later, only one voice hit the high note — Janet.

Blushing, she hid her face as she realized that only she was singing. The entire class burst into applause, cheering for her.

"Wow!" Mr. Carter said with a huge grin. "That was amazing! What's your name, young lady?"

Janet cleared her throat and told him in a soft voice.

Mr. Carter leaned forward. "Sorry?"

"Janet Yarkowsky," she said loudly.

"And you other girls?" He nodded to Ramona and Bunny.

They introduced themselves.

"Have I got a song for you!" He laughed, clapping his hands excitedly. "We've got a competition coming up in October and it calls for three sopranos. Minimal music, just drums and bass, the rest is the vocals. I need one lead, two on harmony and the rest of the chorus behind." He handed the pianist a piece of sheet music.

Her eyes brightened. "You're kidding. For real?"

"What is it, Melanie?" Trina asked.

Instead of answering, the girl started to play. Janet immediately recognized it. She burst into song without thinking about it. It came as naturally to her as breathing. The music filled the hollow, empty places in her. She poured her heart into it, singing *Killing Me Softly* by Roberta Flack.

One of the boys sidled over the the drum set and the men in the bass section improvised a bass line to go with her vocal. Her friends joined her on harmony. The rest sat in awe until they finished. For a moment, the room was silent, then it exploded with applause, cheers and feet pounding the risers.

Janet blushed again, realizing what she'd done. "I'm sorry," she whispered. "I'm so sorry."

She hid her face in her hands until Mr. Carter came over to her. He took her hands, helping her stand.

"I don't think we need to hold auditions for a vocalist, do you?" He appealed to the class.

The entire chorus clapped and cheered again.

"Way to go, Janet!" Trina yelled.

The rest of the room took up the call. Mr. Carter held her hand, encouraging her to take her bow. She did so shyly.

"I'm sorry, I couldn't stop it. I love that song," she said to him. "I didn't mean to mess up auditions."

"You would have gotten it anyway," he said quietly. "You have a beautiful voice."

"Thanks."

Finally, he let her sit down. The rest of class was spent discussing how they could take the song and blow the minds of the judges. Mr. Carter liked the bass section singing instead of using a guitar. He assigned each section the task of adding something new and interesting to the performance.

Diego raised his hand, calling Mr. Carter to the tenor section.

"I had an idea. If the bass section does their thing, we should have the tenors do percussion."

The boys demonstrated, sounding like snare drums, cymbals and bongos. Mr. Carter's eyes lit up.

"Impressive! I like it! Altos, my sweet ladies, what will you be doing?"

"Strings, guitar, flute..." Trina said with a smile.

They also demonstrated. Mr. Carter was thrilled.

"This gets better and better! We're going to blow them away! Tomorrow, have your parts decided and tab written so we can put the pieces together."

"Tomorrow? Mr. C.!" The students complained.

"Okay, by Friday."

More groans.

"Okay, Tuesday."

That got a more enthusiastic response. The bell rang and they headed toward the door. Diego caught up with the girls outside the door.

"I didn't know you could sing like that," he said to Janet. "That was so cool."

"Thanks. I love to sing."

"Me, too. Sets me free," he said quietly with a shy grin.

Janet swallowed hard, blinking back the sudden flood of tears that overwhelmed her. That was exactly what she thought too.

"You should come over today and I can show you how to tab your vocals," Diego told her and Bunny.

"I can't. I have to watch my little sister," Janet said. "But you and Ramona can come over for dinner and we can. Trina and Bunny, too, if you want."

"I'm working tonight," Trina said. "Maybe this weekend?"

"Yeah, we could do that. Bunny?"

"Can't. Already have homework in algebra, can you believe? It's gonna take me hours."

"We can come," Diego said, raising an eyebrow at Ramona.

"Yeah, if we can take some time so genius girl can help me with my biology homework."

"Of course. I told you I'd help. Sorry I can't help with algebra, Bun. Not my thing."

"I know. I'll figure it out eventually."

"What time should we come over?" Ramona asked.

"Six. I have to go to the store and shop for groceries before Sookie gets home."

"I'll give you a ride. We can drop by and get groceries on the way home."

"Really? That would help so much. Thanks."

Diego's friends were irritated that they had to hitch rides with others, but took it in good grace because it was his sister. When they saw Janet was another passenger, they understood even more clearly. More than one lustful thought walked out the door that afternoon.

They made a quick stop at the grocery store and Janet bought the things she needed for the next few days. She'd taken over cooking when she was twelve. Her mother wasn't a very good cook, her meals often inedible. Janet had a talent for it and enjoyed planning meals. Sookie was forced to clean up, something she hated, but their mother had, for once, sided with Janet.

Sookie rode home with their neighbor who had a son her age. He rode with Janet's mom in the morning. They were just pulling into the driveway when Janet arrived.

"Hi, Mrs. Thompson. We had to stop at the store."

"No problem. I picked the kids up and took them for an ice cream. I hope that's okay."

"That's great. Thanks." She turned to her sister. "Did you remember to thank Mrs. Thompson?"

"Yes, *duh*!" She smiled at Mrs. Thompson. "Thanks again, Mrs. T. The ice cream was delicious."

"Bye, Sookie. See you tomorrow, sweetie." She pulled out of the driveway and headed three doors down.

"Who are you?" Sookie demanded of Diego. "You her boyfriend?"

"I'm Ramona's brother," he replied, smiling. He held out his hand to shake hers. "I've heard a lot about you, Sookie."

The little girl eyed his hand distastefully. "Yeah. I bet. She lies a lot." She tossed her dark braids over her shoulder and went in the house.

"That's your sister?" Diego couldn't get over the difference between the two girls.

"Unfortunately. Oh, and I wouldn't hold out your hand near her again. She bites."

Diego shoved his hands in his pockets. He went to the trunk of the car and lifted out the groceries. He got all but two bags. The girls took those and followed him in the kitchen.

"What's for supper?" Ramona asked. "Your fabulous spaghetti? Lasagna?"

"Scarborough Fair Casserole."

"Yeah! I love that!"

"Why you call it that?" Diego asked.

"I use parsley, sage, rosemary and thyme to season it."

"Fun." He smiled as he unpacked the bags. "Can I help?"

"Can you peel potatoes?"

"Give me something hard, huh? Of course I can."

She handed him a peeler, knife and potatoes. He set about peeling and cutting them setting them up for mashed potatoes. Ramona browned the hamburger meat and Janet combined the other ingredients. When everything was ready, she topped it with mashed potatoes and cheese before popping it in the oven.

While they waited for dinner to cook, they sipped root beer and talked about the song. Diego showed the girls what Mr. Carter meant about writing their parts in tab. It was a way of showing the music without notes.

"See, not everyone is good at writing out music, but they can show their work this way and still make it clear," Diego explained. "Even some famous musicians do this."

They continued talking about it over dinner. Sookie didn't even complain about it, she was interested too. After dinner, they cleared the table and Diego volunteered to help Sookie clean up.

"I do it at home all the time. Mom or my sisters cook, my brother and I clean up. Kind of our way of saying thank you to the cook." He glanced at Janet, smiling, his dark eyes twinkling. "Thank you," he said quietly. "It was delicious."

"Janet's a great cook," Ramona said. "She came up with that idea all by herself."

"Really? Wow, that's cool! Makes it that much more special."

"It's just food," Sookie said. "What's the big deal?"

"Because she fixed it with imagination and love," Diego replied. "Anybody can throw food together and call it a meal. Janet thought about it and made something up. So it's cool."

Sookie considered a moment. Nodding, she went back to washing dishes. Janet was stunned. That was the closest she'd come to a compliment from her sister that she'd ever gotten.

At 9:00, Diego and Ramona headed home. Sookie was in bed, so Janet walked them out to the car.

"That was fun," she said. "I'm so glad you came by. I'm pretty limited what I can do since I have to watch fussy pants every night but Saturday and Sunday."

"You're not working this weekend, are you?"

"I work Saturday during the day, but I'm off by three."

"There's a Woody Allen movie playing the matinee at four, would you like to go?"

"Oh, I love Woody Allen! That's *Love and Death*, right?"

"Yeah. It came out a couple months ago. It's really funny."

"You've seen it?" She sounded disappointed.

"I work at the theatre in the projection booth. I haven't seen it in the actual theatre," he said with a grin.

"Yeah, I'd like to go. Is Ramona going too?"

He looked a little embarrassed. "I thought maybe just you and me. That's if you'd like. ... If..."

Janet giggled, putting her hand on his arm. "Don't look so worried, silly. I'd love to go."

"Cool. Should I pick you up at the drive-in?"

"Yeah, that would work great."

"Great. See you tomorrow, Janet."

He leaned toward her as if he were going to kiss her. Janet wasn't sure what vibe she was picking up. It was puzzling. Ramona tapped the horn, making them both jump. Diego cursed at her in Spanish. Janet, who was nearly as fluent as they were, laughed at him.

"I'm sorry..." She giggled. "The expression on your face... Priceless."

Fuming, he pressed his lips shut so he wouldn't say the wrong thing. Pointing at his sister, his jaw worked. Finally, he decided to laugh with the girls.

"Yeah, laugh at me. It's my lot in life," he complained.

"See you tomorrow, Diego. Bye, Ramona. Call me later!"

Her friend nodded, giving a sidelong glance at her brother as he got in the car.

"What was that?" she asked as they headed home.

"What was what?"

"You asked Janet out."

"So?"

"On a *date*."

He glared at her. "Your point?"

"The point is — a date? For real? Diego, what are you thinking?"

"I'm thinking I never realized how much we have in common. She's a nice girl. What's the big deal?"

"Are you cruising for a virgin?"

"Huh?"

"You heard me. I don't stutter."

He shrugged. "I didn't know she was. No. Like I said, she's a nice girl."

"You're not exactly the nicest guy around, Diego."

"Mona, come on! Don't bust my chops! I'm a good guy. I treat my ladies well."

"But so many? Diego, I can't even count the number of girlfriends you've had. And how many of them have you slept with?"

"Not a lot of sleeping involved, Ramona. If it's any of your business, not as many as you might think."

"Girls talk. You think I haven't heard them discussing you? How many of them I've overheard telling their friends how sexy you are? I've heard more about what you can do with your tongue..."

"Enough! Ten. Are you happy?"

"Only ten? You've dated almost twice that many."

"And I've had sex with ten of them."

"Not what they say."

"The others are lying. Who are you going to believe? Me or a bunch of silly girls?"

"You're not above lying."

"If I were gonna lie, wouldn't I make the number *bigger*?"

She sighed. "I don't want Janet hurt. You don't know what her mother is like, Diego. She's not like Mama. She's blames Janet for her dad leaving them. She's a mean woman and don't even get me started on Sookie!"

"All the more reason for her to date me," he said with a proud smile. "I treat my ladies right. I'm not just on the prowl. She could do a lot worse than me. I'd take care of her. I could make her happy."

"I'll allow this on two conditions."

"Wait, you'll *allow* me?"

"I don't stutter. First, you don't push her to have sex."

He started to protest. She shut him up with a look.

"Second, if she agrees to it, you behave like a gentleman, you treat her with respect and you don't dump her right after. Or I promise you, there will be so much pain. . .!"

"Okay," he said petulantly. "Can you believe me when I say that I really like her? I didn't realize until I heard her sing. I didn't know she could... Mona, can I tell you this without you saying anything?"

"Sure, *mi hermano*. we tell each other secrets all the time."

"You can't tell her. And you can't laugh at me."

They did their special handshake that they'd made up when she was five. It was their secret and sealed their pact of silence. Diego pulled up in the driveway, turning off the car before he spoke.

"I heard her sing today and I realized I'm in love with her. I didn't even know... I don't know when it happened... No, I do." He smiled, remembering. "New Year's Eve."

"When you two kissed at midnight?"

He nodded slowly, smiling. "I'm in love with your best friend. Is that weird?"

"I think it's terrific," she said quietly. "Cause she could do a whole lot worse than you, Diego. But I don't think she could do better." She swallowed hard before kissing his cheek. "You treat my friend right, or I'll break your legs."

He laughed, nodding. "I promise."

They got in the house and saw their parents watching TV with their older brother and two younger sisters. Their brother turned down the TV since it was on a commercial.

"Hey, baby brother! Mona!" He hopped up.

"Carlos!" They greeted him with a hug.

"What are you doing here? You didn't tell me he was coming, Mama!" Ramona said.

"We didn't know. He walked in right before dinner."

"You should have called us at Janet's."

Their mother gave them a tight lipped shake of her head. "She needed you there. That mother of hers! And that sister!" She made a disgusted noise. "She needs a little joy. And he'll be here a week."

"How'd you manage that?" Diego asked his brother.

"Got a week's vacation from work and school's on a break. So here I am!"

"Too bad school's started," Diego said with a frown. "We could hang out."

"We can do that this weekend."

"Sunday," Diego said. "We can go to the lake."

"Not Saturday?" Carlos sounded disappointed.

"He can't, he has a date," Ramona said with a toss of her head.

"So, reschedule," his mother said.

"With Janet," Ramona continued with a sly wink. She grabbed a handful of popcorn from a bowl in her sister's lap.

"Oh, really?" Their mother looked interested.

In fact, all eyes in the room were on Diego, ignoring the TV program.

"Yeah. So? It's just a movie."

"Not at the drive-in?" his mother said with a frown.

"No, Mama. At the theatre."

"So, a date..." His mother looked smug.

"It's just a movie... Why's everyone making such a big deal?"

"No reason," their mother said with a satisfied smirk. "Oh, the show's back on." She turned it up.

Annoyed, Diego went to his room. His brother's suitcase was on his old bed. Diego flopped on his own, arms folded under his head. The door opened and Carlos came in.

"Mama shouldn't tease," he said quietly, sitting on the end of Diego's bed. "So, you finally admit you like her. Good for you."

"You know?"

"Bro, I saw the kiss at New Year's."

"I think I'm in love with her, Carlos. Is that crazy?"

"No, man. It's cool that you do."

"I wish she was my age," Diego murmured. "I'd marry her in a heartbeat."

"Get your school first," Carlos said firmly. "I've got friends trying to go to school who are married, some have a baby on the way. It's hard to keep up with marriage and school and kids."

Diego nodded, blinking back tears. "She's got nothin'," he whispered. "Her mom's a bitch. Her little sister's obnoxious. She's got us. We're her family. Is it wrong for me to want to take her away from that?"

"No, brother. It's cool. But it wouldn't be the best thing for you two right now. Think how much harder it would be for her to be married in high school? You've got some married friends, don't you?"

"Yeah. Shotgun weddings."

Carlos nodded. "I know you love her. I can see it all over you. But don't make that mistake, man. You will seriously limit your life."

He was right and Diego knew it. He nodded, accepting Carlos' opinion. Diego couldn't think of a time his older brother had been wrong.

"So, how's school been?"

"Good. Hard to believe I'm starting my third year. Then I start looking at medical schools. If I can get the money..."

"There's scholarships," Diego said. "I been looking. I applied for a bunch already. I go in the counselor's office and apply for anything I can find. They got things for college and medical schools too. I'll find you some addresses. Or you could go talk to Mrs. Chambers. I know she'd help."

"If it weren't for her, I wouldn't be in college," Carlos agreed. "I'll do that."

"It's good to have you home, blood."

"I've missed you, squirt."

Diego laughed loudly. Carlos was three inches shorter and wasn't nearly as broad in the shoulders as his younger, more athletic brother.

"I've missed you, too."

To Be Continued Next Month…

Dellani Oakes is a former A.P. English teacher and photo journalist. Now working as a substitute teacher and Mary Kay consultant, she can give skin care & makeup advice, correct grammar, take pictures and write an article while controlling a classroom full of rowdy third graders.

Dellani was making up stories before she could read. Her first really cohesive work began when her older sister started school. Left to entertain herself, she invented an imaginary friend and would regale her mother with tales of Snowy Green and Rainbow School. These stories paved the way for songs and poems in elementary school and short stories in high school and college.

A college theatre major, Dellani took play writing. It became her new love. Scripts being dialog heavy and character driven, this aspect has followed her into her novel writing. She uses verbal exchanges & sparring as a way of revealing both plot and characterization.

Dellani had to set aside her love of writing when she began working as a teacher. Her creative energies were channeled into writing exams to make her students cry—although this wasn't usually intentional. Unfortunately, between that and motherhood, she didn't have time to write.

However, once her youngest son started school in 2001, she was able to write full time. Her first published novel, "Indian Summer", was published in 2008 by Second Wind Publishing. Also from Second Wind, her second novel, "Lone Wolf" makes its debut soon. "Lone Wolf" is the first in her science-fiction series.

When asked recently how she thought of all those stories, she replied: "There are more ideas in my head than I can get written down. I'll have to live forever."

Dellani wrote: "Every second Monday at 4:00 PM Eastern, I host Dellani's Tea Time. I talk to authors & illustrators of children's and young adult's books. On every fourth Wednesday at 1:00 PM Eastern, I host What's Write for Me. On this show, I talk to authors who write for adults. I think it's safe to say that we take ourselves VERY seriously and we aren't allowed to laugh at all. Never ever, ever! She is the author of *Lone Wolf and Indian Summer* and *Ninja Tattoo*. Find her at http://dellanioakes.wordpress.com/ and writersanctuary.blogspot.com

CONTRIBUTORS

Barbara Watkins

Barbara Watkins resides in Missouri with her husband and loyal boxweiler, Hooch. In her writings, she loves to evoke a false sense of security and expectations, as she leads her reader into a world of the unknown. Her articles on various subjects, short stories, and poetry, have appeared in 2008 *New York Skyline Review*, and several on-line publications. *Cold Coffee Magazine* accepted her article, "A Testament To Poets," for their second issue released in print and is available online at *Cold Coffee Magazine.*

In 2010, Watkins collaborated with New Zealand director, Dimi Nakov, on a screenplay for a short movie titled "BlindSide." Her name appears at the film's end credits for voice-over monologue. "BlindSide" was accepted into the Cannes short film corner as part of the 65th Festival de Cannes as well as the 7th Cyprus International Film Festival 2012, and many more prestigious film festivals.

Many of her short stories and novella, *Thorns of an Innocent Soul*, have been optioned to New Zealand film production company, Zodiac Entertainment, for screenplay adaptation to film.

Previous Publications: *Mortal Abomination — Awaken Spirit — Hollowing Screams — Six-Pack of Blood* (co-author, Betty Dravis) *Six-Pack of Fear* (co-author, Betty Dravis). Anthologies include, *Hope Whispers* (compiled by Lynn C. Johnston) *Live Life: The Daydreamer's Journal* (compiled by Sir Ricky McGentleman) *Satan's Holiday*, an anthology of scary stories (compiled by Yvonne Mason) and *Writing Tips From Authors* (compiled by Patti Roberts.)

Visit her website: www.barbarawatkins.net

Brian Hayden, author

Brian Hayden was born in Chicago, Illinois, in 1954 into a middle-class, blue-collar, Jewish family. He is the middle child with a brother one year older senior, and a sister two years younger. In 1961, his family moved to the suburbs of Los Angeles, California. He is a second generation, American-born son of Austrian and English grandparents on my father's side, and Polish and Russian grandparents on my mother's side. I enlisted in the United States Air Force in 1972, and was finally medically discharged in July of 1990.

He published his earliest book in 1999, titled *Using Strategic and Tactical Planning to Make Your Veterinary Practice More Profitable.* During that period, he wrote five scripts for educational videos. Then, in February of 2011, he published his memoir, *Death: Living To Talk About It.* On August 20, 2012, he published his first work of fiction, *Five Short Stories and Twelve Poems.* Now, after more than two years in the works, *Road To Transplant*, his sequel to the memoir was published in 2012. He continues to write both fiction and nonfiction and maintains a weekly blog.

Christoph Fischer, author

Christoph Fischer was born in Germany in 1970 but moved on to the UK in the early 1990s where he is still resident today. *The Luck of The Weissensteiners* is his first published work and concerns a Jewish Family in Slovakia during the 1930s and 1940s. *Sebastian* his second book about a young handicapped man in Vienna in the 1910s was published in May 2013. He has written several other novels, which are in the later stages of editing and finalization. Both of his book have received critical acclaim and have entered the indie tribe fiction charts and the Amazon charts for Jewish Fiction.

He is currently on of the Top 1% of reviewers on Goodreads and #1727 reviewer on Amazon.

His recommendations and reviews can be found at http://writerchristophfischer.wordpress.com/ and http://www.christophfischerbooks.com

David and Faith McDonald

David S. McDonald is a minister, along with his wife, Faith of Whole Heart Abundance ministries (W.H.A.M.,INC.) of Chattanooga, Tenn. They have two children Shane Isbill and Shannon Isbill also of Chattanooga and four grandchildren: Christian, Ashlyn and Jared, Elise. David has widely read from many disciplines of life and study, incorporating these bodies of knowledge into the stories he writes. His writing influences also include such writers of fiction as Sir Arthur Conan Doyle, Isacc Asimov, Theodore Sturgeon, Ray Bradbury, Stephen King and many others. He is also a student of all religions and philosophies. Though, a devout Christian, David takes an eclectic approach to world views, respecting all belief systems and the right of all to freely choose how they believe. Joy, faith, understanding, patience, love, forgiveness and integrity with God's strength lead him along his own path. He and his wife, Faith's heart's desire is to illuminate minds and heal hearts with the wisdom of peace, thereby, alleviating much of the World's suffering. Reason shall and must prevail.

David Workman, author

David Workman's debut novel, *Absolute Authority,* hit the shelves in early 2012 to roaring acclaim. A native St. Louisan, he was recently named by local television station KMOV as one of St. Louis' Top 5 New Authors. Along with writing novels, David has spent most of his 20-year writing career hammering out advertising and marketing copy for companies large and small, including his current gig as the lead contest specialist for a major athletic shoe company. His second novel, a sequel, is scheduled for a winter 2013 release. Find him on Facebook.

Dellani Oakes, author

Dellani Oakes is a former A.P. English teacher and photojournalist. Now working as a substitute teacher and Mary Kay consultant, she can give skin care & makeup advice, correct grammar, take pictures and write an article while controlling a classroom full of rowdy third graders.

Dellani is the author of *Lone Wolf and Indian Summer* and *Ninja Tattoo.* Find her at http://dellanioakes.wordpress.com/ and writersanctuary.blogspot.com

Donald Riggio, author

Donald Riggio was born and raised in the Bronx, New York and has had a deep and enduring love of rock and roll music since he was a boy. His love of writing is equally enduring as is illustrated in his success as a short story and technical writer over the years.

He combined his two passions with the publication of his first novel, *Seven-Inch Vinyl: A Rock and Roll Novel,* in 2011. That book became a #1 Kindle Best Seller in the music category as did the sequel, *Beyond Vinyl: The Rock and Roll Saga Continues* published in 2012.

He also hosts a hugely successful Facebook page, where he and his 3,500+ friends discuss, post pictures, rock and roll song links and information 24/7. He invites everyone to join him.

Mr. Riggio lives in Las Vegas, Nevada, where he is currently writing the third book in his trilogy, When Gold Turns to Gray.

Fran Lewis, Author, reviewer, educator, talk show host, creator of M.J. Magazine

Fran Lewis: Fran worked in the NYC Public Schools as the Reading and Writing Staff Developer for over 36 years. She has three masters Degrees and a PD in Supervision and Administration. Currently, she is a member of Who's Who of America's Teachers and Who's Who of America's Executives from Cambridge. In addition, she is the author of three children's books and a fourth that has just been published on Alzheimer's disease in order to honor her mom and help create more awareness for a cure. The title of my new Alzheimer's book is Memories are Precious: Alzheimer's Journey; Ruth's story and Sharp as a Tack and Scrambled Eggs Which Describes Your Brain? Fran is also the author of Faces Behind the Stones, Bad Choices and M.J. Magazine an E-Magazine dedicated to the memory of her sister

Marcia Joyce. She is also a member of Continental's Who's Who of America's Executives and Professionals and the author of 11 titles. She is presently working on creating a second radio show called Chat Time with Fran Lewis on Blog Talk Radio the Red River Network and adding more outstanding shows on the World of Ink Network. Her show Book Discussion is heard all over the world and she has many listeners.

She was the musical director for shows in her school and ran the school's newspaper. Fran writes reviews for authors upon request and for several other sites. You can read some of my reviews on Ezine.comand on ijustfinished.com under the name Gabina. Here is the link to her radio show www.blogtalkradio.com

Karen Vaughan, author

Karen H. Vaugan is a first-time author who enjoys reading and writing. She is a part of Class 1983 at Applewood Heights Secondary School in Mississauga, ON. She is married with one daughter, and four stepchildren. She has two cats at home. She has a warped sense of humor and sees the lighter side of things.

She is the co-author of Dead on Arrival (Julie Faulkner), Daytona Dead, Over Her Dead Body and Dead Comic Standing. Books may be purchased from her website at www.KarenVaughan.info

Kenneth Weene, author

Life itches and torments Kenneth Weene like pesky flies. Annoyed, he picks up a pile of paper to slap at the buzzing and often whacks himself on the head. Each whack is another story. At least having half-blinded himself, he has learned to not wave the pencil about. Ken will, however, write on until the last gray cell has retreated and there are no longer these strange ideas demanding his feeble efforts. So many poems, stories, novels; and more to come.

Learn more about Ken at http://www.kennethweene.com and find Ken's novels in print, e-format, and audio.

Mark Bouton, author

Mark Bouton writes mystery and nonfiction books. He worked for the FBI and "nabbed killers, kidnappers, and bank robbers." He also played a key role in solving the Oklahoma City bombing. He uses his experiences to inform his writing. His books move fast, with lots of action, humor, strange characters, and striking plot twists.

He has also written a nonfiction book about how to tell when someone's lying. He has learned to read faces, bodies, and voices to avoid being fooled ever again.

John Emil Augustine

John Emil Augustine is an author at Master Koda Select Publishing. He toured in his twenties and early thirties with local and national acts; writing, arranging, and performing on the road with well-known Jazz, Blues, Gospel, Reggae, Post Funk, Prog Rock, and Folk Rock groups. John has also been a landscaper, mail carrier, English professor, and forklift operator. He currently lives in Minneapolis, MN with his wife and four boys.

Learn more about him by visiting these websites: http://masterkodaselectpublishing.com and http://www.johnemilaugustine.com

Mark Rubenstein, author

Mark Rubinstein was born in Brooklyn, New York. He dreamed of playing baseball for the Brooklyn Dodgers since his all-time hero was the Dodgers' first baseman Gil Hodges. Rubinstein played high school baseball and ran track. His love of sports led him to read sports fiction, and soon he became a voracious reader, developing an enduring love for all kinds of novels.

He graduated from New York University with a degree in business administration. He then served in the army and ended up as a field medic tending to paratroopers of the 82nd Airborne Division. He was so taken with these experiences that after his discharge, he re-entered NYU as a premed student.

He entered medical school at the State University of New York's Downstate Medical Center. As a medical student, he developed an interest in psychiatry, discovering in that specialty the same thing he realized in reading fiction: every patient has a compelling story to tell. He became a board-certified psychiatrist practicing in New York City.

In addition to running his private practice he developed an interest in forensic psychiatry because the drama and conflict of the cases and courtrooms tapped into his personality style. He also taught psychiatric residents, interns, psychologists, and social workers at New York Presbyterian Hospital and became a clinical assistant professor at Cornell University's medical school.

Before turning to fiction, Rubinstein coauthored five medical self-help books: *The First Encounter: The Beginnings in Psychotherapy* (Jason Aronson); *The Complete Book of Cosmetic Facial Surgery* (Simon and Schuster); *New Choices: the Latest Options in Treating Breast Cancer* (Dodd Mead); *Heartplan: A Complete Program for Total Fitness of Heart & Mind* (McGraw-Hill), and *The Growing Years: A Guide to Your Child's Emotional Development from Birth to Adolescence* (Atheneum).

Rubinstein lives in Connecticut with his wife and as many dogs as she will allow in the house. He still practices psychiatry and is busily writing more novels. *Mad Dog House*, his first novel, was named a Finalist for the 2012 *ForeWord Reviews* Book of the Year Award (Thriller & Suspense).

Martha Cheves, author

Writes cookbooks and *Stir, Laugh, Repeat* is her first book. Her cookbooks are different and use simple recipes with common ingredients found in most kitchens. She says, "No matter how many mistakes you make, never give up." When I was around 6 years old I talked my mother into letting me make the biscuits for dinner. They came out just a bit hard. In fact they were so hard that my oldest brother hit my youngest brother with one and he ended up with a black eye. Now those were some really BAD biscuits. But I didn't give up and I now make deliciously light and fluffy biscuits that people actually ask for."

Maxine Horton Bringenberg, editor

Maxine Horton Bringenberg was raised in the mountains of northeastern Kentucky, in a little town on the Ohio River, and calls herself a "river rat." Life has allowed her to live in many locations, including Atlanta and Florida's Gulf Coast, but she currently resides in a suburb of Columbus, Ohio with her husband, two grown children, and four cats. Much of her adult life has been spent working with adults with special needs, and also in the health care field. But since childhood, Maxine has had a love of the written word, and a few years ago was delighted to be given the opportunity to edit mostly fictional books. While she has not yet published a book of her own, the authors she works with now are a constant source of inspiration, and she hopes to find her muse soon.

R.J. Ellory, Best selling author

R.J. Ellory is the author of *Three Days in Chicagoland,* which focuses on the brutal murder of a young girl in Chicago in 1956, as told from three different viewpoints: The Sister, The Cop and The Killer. His other books are *Candlemoth, Ghostheart, A Quiet Vendetta, City of Lies, A Quiet Belief in Angels, A Simple Act of Violence, The Anniversary Man, Saints of New York, Bad Signs, A Dark and Broken Heart, The Devil and the River.* Visit his website: *www.RJEllory.com*

Susan Ross, Children's Book Reviewer

Susan is a former school secretary who worked over twenty years in the New York City Public School System. She is an avid reader and enjoys reading to her three grandchildren. Her main goal is to encourage young children to read many different types of books. Susan's reviews will hopefully encourage parents and young children to read more and choose some of the books that she spotlighted as her best picks in this issue.

CHECK BACK AT YOUR FAVORITE E-RETAILER FOR NEW EDITIONS EVERY OTHER MONTH!

I hope you enjoy reading, and we encourage comments and contributors.

- To be considered for a position as one of MJ Magazine's book reviewers, please contact Fran at riffyone@optonline.net and use **I'd like to be an MJ Magazine book reviewer** as your subject line.
- If you would like to contribute an article, please send the article, a photograph of yourself in .jpg format and a short bio using the subject line **Article for MJ Magazine** to Fran at riffyone@optonline.net (sending a submission does not guarantee it will be run).
- If you would like to have your book reviewed by *MJ Magazine*, please contact Fran (riffyone@optonline.net) for information about eligibility, requirements and mailing information using the subject line **MJ Magazine Book Review Information.**
- Tell us what you think about our first issue, what you'd like to see in subsequent issues, etc. by emailing riffyone@optonline.net with the subject line **Comments for MJ Magazine.**

Until next time …

www.ingramcontent.com/pod-product-compliance
Lightning Source LLC
Chambersburg PA
CBHW082102090726
47910CB00008B/2563